Becoming an Outstanding Personal Tutor

You might also like the following FE books from Critical Publishing

A Complete Guide to the Level 4 Certificate in Education and Training, 2nd edition
Lynn Machin, Duncan Hindmarch, Sandra Murray and Tina Richardson
978-1-910391-09-9

A Complete Guide to the Level 5 Diploma in Education and Training
Lynn Machin, Duncan Hindmarch, Sandra Murray and Tina Richardson
978-1-909682-53-5

The A-Z Guide to Working in Further Education
Jonathan Gravells and Susan Wallace
978-1-909330-85-6

Equality and Diversity in Further Education
Sheine Peart
978-1-909330-97-9

Inclusion in Further Education
Lydia Spenceley
978-1-909682-05-4

The Professional Teacher in Further Education
Keith Appleyard and Nancy Appleyard
978-1-909682-01-6

Reflective Teaching and Learning in Further Education
Nancy Appleyard and Keith Appleyard
978-1-909682-85-6

Teaching and Supporting Adult Learners
Jackie Scruton and Belinda Ferguson
978-1-909682-13-9

Teaching in Further Education: The Inside Story
Susan Wallace
978-1-909682-73-3

Understanding the Further Education Sector: A Critical Guide to Policies And Practices
Susan Wallace
978-1-909330-21-4

Our titles are also available in a range of electronic formats. To order please go to our website www.criticalpublishing.com or contact our distributor, NBN International, 10 Thornbury Road, Plymouth PL6 7PP, telephone 01752 202301 or email orders@nbninternational.com.

Becoming an Outstanding Personal Tutor

Supporting Learners through Personal Tutoring and Coaching

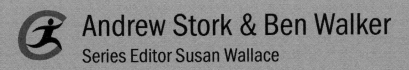

Andrew Stork & Ben Walker

Series Editor Susan Wallace

FURTHER EDUCATION

First published in 2015 by Critical Publishing Ltd

British Library Cataloguing in Publication Data
A CIP record for this book is available from the British Library

ISBN: 978-1-910391-05-1

This book is also available in the following e-book formats:

MOBI ISBN: 978-1-910391-06-8
EPUB ISBN: 978-1-910391-07-5
Adobe e-book: 978-1-910391-08-2

Cover and text design by Greensplash Limited
Project Management by Out of House Publishing
Printed and bound in Great Britain by 4edge Limited, Hockley, Essex
on FSC accredited paper

Critical Publishing
152 Chester Road
Northwich
CW8 4AL
www.criticalpublishing.com

Contents

Meet the authors

Andrew Stork

I am a marketing lecturer and teacher trainer who has co-responsibility for the personal tutoring and coaching of learners at The Sheffield College. I previously worked in marketing management and consultancy roles before retraining. Since then, I have taught in secondary schools and further education colleges delivering business education and teacher training courses. I have a wide range of experience training, mentoring and supporting teachers and personal tutors as module leader on PGCE and certificate of education courses, as well as undertaking various curriculum leadership and quality roles, such as advanced practitioner, observer and trainee teacher mentor. I am currently undertaking research into how coaching conversations help learners with the University of Sunderland's Centre for Excellence in Teacher Training, funded by the Education and Training Foundation.

Ben Walker

I was a full-time English lecturer at Chesterfield College for several years before becoming head of department for English at The Sheffield College. Currently, I have co-responsibility for the personal tutoring and coaching of learners at The Sheffield College and I teach on the PGCE and certificate of education courses. As module leader on these courses, and through quality roles such as observer, I have trained, mentored and supported teachers and personal tutors. I am currently undertaking research into how coaching conversations help learners with the University of Sunderland's Centre for Excellence in Teacher Training, funded by the Education and Training Foundation.

Authors' websites

The self assessment systems in this book can be downloaded free of charge from the publisher's website www.criticalpublishing.com or from the authors' websites.

Andrew Stork: www.andrewstork.co.uk

Ben Walker: www.benwwalker.co.uk

Meet the series editor

Susan Wallace

I am Emeritus Professor of Education at Nottingham Trent University where, for many years, part of my role was to support learning on the initial training courses for teachers in the further education (FE) sector. I taught in the sector myself for ten years, including on BTEC programmes and basic skills provision. My particular interest is in the motivation and behaviour of students in FE, and in mentoring and the ways in which a successful mentoring relationship can support personal and professional development. I have written a range of books, mainly aimed at teachers and student teachers in the sector; and I enjoy hearing readers' own stories of FE, whether it's by email or at speaking engagements and conferences.

Acknowledgements

We would like to thank:

- the wonderful personal tutors who so impressively carry out the important work we have written about in this book;

- our fellow learner success managers;

- Shaun Lincoln for ongoing encouragement, help and wise advice, and for his kind permission to use Table 6.3, Potential solution talk and problem talk questions, from Lincoln (2004) *Solution-Focused Coaching Training Materials*;

- senior management at The Sheffield College;

- Julia Morris and Sue Wallace for their continuing advice and support, and Sue for her kind permission to use Figures 1.2 and 1.4, taken from Wallace, S and Gravells, J (2007) *Mentoring* Second Edition. Exeter: Learning Matters;

- Jason, for getting Ben into FE in the first place;

- Lorna, Petra and our families, for getting us through when it was difficult, being patient in our absence and for their unwavering support.

A note on terminology

In the world of education, the terms 'learner' and 'student' are used interchangeably. We have used 'learner' simply because this is currently Ofsted's preferred term, but 'student' could just as easily be used for the situations the book covers.

Dedication

To Lorna, Josh and Jake. Always.
AS

To Jenn, and in loving memory of Arthur.
BW

Introduction

Who this book is for

You may have picked up this book because you are a trainee teacher, either in-service or pre-service, within further education (FE), a sixth-form college or a school. It could be that you are an experienced teacher or specialised personal tutor within one of these sectors. Or, you may work within education but be employed purely within learner support. Equally, you could be a manager within education who oversees support of learners or curriculum delivery. More widely, you may be employed in one of the many different learner-facing roles such as teaching assistant or within additional support. It is important to state that whichever one of these describes you best – and there will be other related roles that come under a slightly different description to those mentioned – this book is relevant to you. As you will see from the next section, the book has been written with the trainee teacher uppermost in our minds; however, it is not exclusive to this audience. Support to learners, which is at the core of the book, is delivered in many ways and through a variety of roles so, indeed, we can say that anyone who works with learners in any way will find this book useful to carry out their work as effectively as they can.

Your first activity

» *In terms of your personal tutor role, think about your level of knowledge and how effective you feel you are. On a scale of one to ten, with one being very little knowledge and very limited effectiveness and ten being extensive knowledge with highly effective practice, where are you on the scale? Hang on to this number because we will be revisiting it at the end of the book.*

Why you need this book

The life of the teacher – and particularly a trainee teacher – can seem like a whirlwind. In fact, for me, being a trainee teacher was one of the most intense experiences of my life. While for most of us, once we're an experienced practitioner the whirlwind lessens somewhat, at the beginning of our teaching career it often feels like gale force ten is the norm. One of my clearest memories of being a trainee teacher was how much more quickly the day passed compared to in my previous job, such was the activity and concentration required for this new occupation; preparation, marking, creating resources, working with new colleagues of all types and, at the centre of it all, teaching learners, with the classroom being one of the most rewarding but challenging places to be.

Through all of this, along with the myriad of things I had to think about, something was nagging at the back of my mind. What about personal support of learners and tutorials? Even though I knew it was a duty, or aspect of the role, it didn't seem particularly high on anyone's agenda, and given the demands of delivering a curriculum subject, I was no different. If it was given any attention, both on the teacher training course and on the placement itself, it seemed minimal at best and, in any case, my curriculum duties certainly took precedence. It was also something different to the rest of my teaching. This support didn't have a qualification attached. Any content to be covered, either with individual learners or in a group tutorial, was vague and undefined. Supporting learners may have been mentioned, but there didn't seem to be any guidance on how I was supposed to carry it out. Did this matter? If the whole thing was 'looser', surely time allocated to this support was the easy part, a time to be more relaxed and take refuge from the whirlwind? That thought soon disappeared after trying to carry out personal support of learners early in my first few weeks of teaching. Its very lack of definition made it *less* relaxing rather than more. There didn't seem to be enough significant things to do, in both the wider sense of supporting learners and the designated tutorial session itself. The learners knew this and in some cases were very quick to state that to me openly! I hadn't heard much about coaching at this point, or if I had, I hadn't made the link with personal tutoring. The guidance that this book provides would have been most welcome.

Of course, your first experiences of personal tutoring may be more positive in terms of clarity of expectation and content. However, so that personal tutoring practice, which is so crucial to learners' success, is not sidelined, the book's focus is to develop this, interlinking it with coaching, alongside curriculum delivery.

Furthermore, the book's purpose is to provide a highly effective approach for delivering personal tutoring and coaching, which, given this is an underdeveloped area, is much needed by pre-service and in-service trainee teachers and existing practitioners alike.

It will also act as a 'toolkit' for you by providing the tools to achieve excellence in personal tutoring and coaching to meet learner needs. In turn, these key elements will positively impact upon the key performance indicators of your educational institution which, whether you are in training, newly qualified or experienced, you will no doubt have heard a lot about: retention, success, attendance and punctuality, value-added and internal progression.

It is also important to reinforce that the book should not only be viewed as relevant to your personal tutor role. In other words, since personal tutoring values and skills are central to successful teaching as a whole, the book will inform your whole practice. By comprehensively covering these aspects, it provides an invaluable resource in what is currently an under-resourced area.

Why else is personal tutoring so important?

The ever-changing and diverse backgrounds of learners, along with the challenges these present, mean understanding learners individually is the best way to support them to succeed. As explained by Harriet Swain in her article The Personal Tutor:

> *The diverse backgrounds of today's students mean that the role of the personal tutor is more important than ever. As the student population expands and changes, traditional expectations of the tutor's role may no longer be accurate.*
>
> (Swain, 2008, online)

She doesn't discuss what these traditional expectations may be, but I can surmise that these are similar 'expectations' to those I experienced at the beginning of my teaching career. Although, as we've seen, there were hardly any expectations to talk of, other than a rather vague one to 'check-in' with learners on a weekly basis in a tutorial session. However, this simply doesn't cut it when faced with the challenging and complex individual issues that learners present. For example, we have worked with departments within which between a quarter and a third of the learners lived independently, and within colleges where the proportion of learners with additional support needs made up a quarter of the entire full-time 16–18-year-old learner population. This is not to say that only these types of learner cohorts present problems to be addressed. Whatever the make-up of your learner population, you will be faced with complex issues.

In the face of these, a new set of expectations for the personal tutor role is needed. Moreover, they are needed to stretch and challenge more-able learners. Whether this is through individualised tracking and monitoring (Chapter 4), identifying and supporting 'at risk' and 'vulnerable' learners (Chapter 4) or taking a positive approach to disciplinary (Chapter 5), the new expectations of the personal tutor will be set out clearly for you.

By drawing on our experience of working with varied cohorts of learners and staff, the book will comprehensively cover the tools and skills you will need in order to provide outstanding personal tutoring.

Why is personal tutoring so crucial in the current educational climate?

No doubt you will have heard about Ofsted more than a few times already. Is there a link between inspection and the values and skills we are exploring in this book? Most certainly. The Common Inspection Framework (CIF) of September 2015 makes greater reference to learner support and these types of skills and approaches.

So, how does Ofsted recognise these elements in institutions that are doing really well? The following statements are extracts from Swindon College's outstanding Ofsted report in 2013:

> *Planning for individual learners' needs is very good. Initial assessment, not only of literacy and numeracy but also of social needs, is carried out promptly and the results are used well by staff to guide their teaching and support activities.*
>
> (Ofsted, 2013, p 3)

> *Course tutors and student experience managers work together very effectively to design and implement pastoral and educational packages of support that enable vulnerable learners, and those at risk of leaving, to remain on programme and succeed. This exceptional support is balanced with clear boundaries and expectations of learners, the use of good action plans, and disciplinary procedures if needed.*
>
> (Ofsted, 2013, p 4)

> *The many well-resourced, well-structured and planned elements of the college care system link very effectively to provide a seamless support system that helps learners make good progress or guides them if personal circumstances intervene to hinder their learning.*
>
> (Ofsted, 2013, p 3)

The key phrases are:

- *individual learners' needs;*
- *social needs;*
- *college care system;*
- *seamless support system;*
- *personal circumstances*

and a longer key extract:

- *... pastoral and educational packages of support that enable vulnerable learners, and those at risk of leaving, to remain on programme and succeed.*

These highlight the importance of developing the *whole* learner, not just their academic prowess, in order to prepare them for their lives outside the classroom, which is central to the personal tutoring approach. This is further brought into focus by the demand from employers for good employability skills. Moreover, the extracts express the new expectations of personal tutoring, both for the individual carrying this out as well as for how the institution organises the role within its structure.

The profile and importance of personal tutoring has been further enhanced by the recently approved National Occupational Standards for Personal Tutoring which can be mapped to the CIF and are explored further in Chapter 4 (key activities) and Chapter 9 (measuring impact).

The change in language, as shown by the Ofsted report extracts, from what we may call the *academic* to *social*, or rather the addition of the latter to the former, shows the many and varied roles that the modern teacher carries out. Indeed, it is not uncommon to hear comments from teachers such as 'I feel more like a social worker some days'. We could add to this list of roles. How about counsellor, therapist, personal organiser, referee, mediator, advocate, careers adviser...? Depending on the stage of your career, you either may not know yet that these skills will be required or know only too well the many hats that the modern-day teacher and personal tutor must wear.

The current educational context then, is one where the increasing diversity of learners' needs demand that our professional skills be multi-faceted; and this is reinforced by Ofsted expectations. This 'multi-facetedness' is underlined by the fact that the context is also one where specialised services are often the first to be cut as a result of government austerity measures, so it is we, as teachers and personal tutors, who must provide this nurturing and support service to learners. Moreover, the personal tutor can play a key role in stretching and challenging any learner to achieve more. So, in terms of both enabling higher achievement as well as providing essential nurturing and support, this book will provide you with the knowledge and skills needed to deliver this service.

How does this book link to your teacher training or current role?

If you are a trainee teacher, the link between the book's content and your teacher training qualification is clear when you consider that personal tutoring, coaching and supporting learners are areas that are implicit within your qualification. Moreover, it will contextualise this content into real-world educational situations that you will come across in-service, on placement or in your day-to-day encounters with learners. If you are a newly qualified or experienced practitioner, it will provide an in-depth overview of the role of personal tutoring, coaching and supporting learners.

Of course, hopefully you can see that principles to be covered are not restricted to teachers but also are invaluable to those in other learner-facing roles, for example dedicated support staff (teaching assistants, additional support) and, as such, are transferable. As we mentioned at the outset, the skills are delivered in many ways and sometimes through different roles – indeed, by anyone who works with learners in any capacity.

Chapter summaries

Chapter 1 sets the scene for the whole book by answering the question 'what is a personal tutor?' It does this, firstly, by exploring the natural overlap between outstanding teaching and personal tutor practice, along with defining our term and looking at the relationship between personal tutoring and coaching. Some different theoretical models are used to further understand the role, as well as how it fits into organisational structures.

In the first part of Chapter 2 we outline and explore the core values of the personal tutor through examples of these in action. We discuss the core skills in the second part of the chapter, differentiating these from the core values by clarifying that values are able to be seen through actions, whereas core skills are the actions themselves. The necessary boundaries between you and the learner, and between learners themselves, are explored in Chapter 3.

Chapters 4 and 5 are lengthier chapters which comprehensively cover the toolkit you need for providing outstanding support to learners. We have named these 'the learner experience' since, by putting these tools into action, you will be covering all aspects of a learner's experience. Firstly, we define the overall aims of using these tools: retention of learners and standards of attendance, behaviour and completion ('ABC'). We have divided them into key activities (Chapter 4) and key procedures (Chapter 5) with the following topics being covered: the tracking and monitoring of learners; one-to-one tutorials (we refer to these as 'one-to-ones' throughout); group tutorial planning and teaching; disciplinary – a positive approach; right course review; internal and external progression; working with learners who have additional support needs; and safeguarding.

In Chapters 6 to 9 we build on the toolkit to develop your higher level support skills through exploring solution-focused coaching (Chapter 6), observation (Chapter 7), reflective practice (Chapter 8) and measuring impact (Chapter 9).

Finally, in Chapter 10 we look at the 'bigger picture'. This allows you to explore and prioritise your own professional development activities as well as to consider the development activities of the institution you work within and how you could influence positive organisational change.

About the book and how to use it

We hope the experience of reading the book will be similar to being taught, with the added bonus that you can dip in and out of the lesson since each chapter can be used in isolation. Therefore, it can be used as a reference book or read in sequence as a whole.

Chapter content includes aims, case studies and examples which are linked to critical thinking activities. All examples are real. However, names of people and departments have been changed for confidentiality. Although examples are taken from FE colleges, they are transferable to different contexts, including sixth-form colleges or schools, making this book vital for anyone working with learners in a learning capacity.

At the end of each chapter there is a chapter summary, a learning checklist to check your understanding of key points, and critical reflections which pose some key questions for you to answer in note or essay form and prompt you to critically analyse your practice.

In addition, at the end of each chapter (from Chapter 2 onwards), there is an individual and institutional self-assessment system which allows you to score your own performance and that of your educational institution on the key theme of each chapter. The rating will be measured against minimum standard, bronze, silver, gold and platinum levels, enabling you to reach a cumulative score and level at the end of the book.

References

OFSTED (2013) *Learning and Skills Inspection Report; Swindon College General Further Education College.* [online] Available at: www.swindon-college.ac.uk/sites/www.swindon-college.ac.uk/files/130849__1.PDF [accessed May 2015].

Swain, H (2008) *The Personal Tutor.* [online] Available at: www.timeshighereducation.co.uk/news/the-personal-tutor/210049.article [accessed May 2015].

1 What is a personal tutor?

Chapter aims

This chapter helps you to:

- explore the natural overlap between outstanding teaching and personal tutor practice;

- define the personal tutor;

- explore the useful relationship between personal tutoring and coaching;

- consider different theoretical models and apply these to different situations;

- recognise the useful qualities and attributes of personal tutoring within different situations and create actions to improve your practice;

- understand different institutional models of personal tutoring and evaluate their relative advantages and disadvantages.

Setting the scene

How outstanding personal tutoring principles lead to outstanding teaching

The principles of being an outstanding teacher are very similar, if not the same in most instances, as the principles of being an outstanding personal tutor. For example, both the teacher and personal tutor demonstrate a commitment to learners through respecting their uniqueness and individuality and therefore provide appropriate learning experiences as well as aiming to motivate and inspire learners to achieve their potential. Personal tutoring principles are ones that most trainee and experienced teachers use many times throughout their working day. Even though these are principles that learners find particularly helpful, they tend to be the least written about and are not always covered in teacher training.

So, what are these principles? We use the phrase *outstanding personal tutoring principles* as the umbrella term which includes all of the numerous aspects covered within this book, from values and skills through to key activities and measuring impact, together with everything in between. Your teacher training will show you how to plan and teach a good lesson, which is of course vital. However, it is important to explore how other complementary approaches, which help learners succeed, can be learnt and mastered.

Good teachers and good teaching aim to put each learner at the centre of everything, whether that is when planning a lesson, marking a piece of homework or even having a departmental meeting with colleagues. In today's modern, fast-paced, target-driven and ever-changing educational landscape, teachers, whether you like it or not, are expected to offer more to a learner's success than just traditional classroom delivery. Whatever your methods, you are trying to help learners to get from point A to point B, but more quickly than they could do by themselves. Point B is learner success, though as you will already have found out, 'success' for each learner looks very different and, if we are honest, probably *should* look very different. This is where the outstanding personal tutoring principles will enable you to help your learners achieve more, not only in terms of passing an exam or achieving a good grade on a piece of coursework, but also in terms of developing the *whole* learner, one who can confidently overcome all of the many and varied challenges they encounter.

The focus on a greater holistic approach to education has also been reinforced outside education by, for example, The Confederation of British Industry (CBI), which states that '*we need an education and skills system that supports and encourages the holistic development of young people, with a focus on attitudes and behaviours as well as knowledge and skills*', and for this to happen they would like to see '*a framework* [Ofsted] *that places more equal weight on this wider personal development as on academic progress*' and they also propose placing personal development as a separate graded judgement (Confederation of British Industry, 2014, online). This has, in part, come to pass with the 2015 Common Inspection Framework.

As you read through the book, you will find that in your role as a personal tutor you are well placed to be able to contribute to this more holistic approach to developing your learners (see Figure 1.1).

It is important to understand that the line between outstanding teaching and personal tutoring principles do overlap and naturally become blurred as you face different situations and challenges both within and outside the classroom. The likelihood is that the personal tutoring principles will be performed alongside your curriculum teaching and vice versa.

When working with learners for the first time as trainee teachers, we have a tendency to be overly analytical and critical of our teaching practice. This is natural and also not such a bad thing in moderation because it shows that you are keen to get it right and to improve. The key to becoming an outstanding personal tutor is like many things in teaching (and life): practice, practice, practice. If you continue to apply the personal tutoring principles in different situations and with different types of learners and reflect on the impact, then you will quickly move from being an intrepid beginner to becoming an outstanding personal tutor.

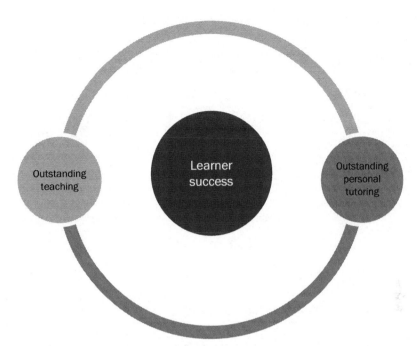

Figure 1.1 *Learner success: outstanding teaching and personal tutoring*

The definition of the personal tutor

Here, we define the personal tutor. But remember, in this book we shall explore what it means to be an *outstanding* personal tutor.

> *The personal tutor is one who improves the intellectual and academic ability, and nurtures the emotional well-being, of learners through individualised, holistic support.*

What constitutes emotional well-being is discussed later in the book.

In addition to this definition, we want to bring in the highly important and valuable element of coaching. Personal tutoring and coaching can be seen as separate, but the model of the outstanding personal tutor includes coaching elements within it. In order to understand this more fully, we will analyse scenarios later in the chapter as well as dedicating a full chapter to solution-focused coaching (Chapter 6).

Personal tutoring and coaching: dictionary definitions and history of the terms

There are many definitions of coaching in existence but very few of personal tutoring. Viewing the 'stock' dictionary definitions of the terms and their derivation (source and original meanings) aids understanding. The *Concise Oxford English Dictionary* and the online etymology dictionary give us the following definitions and derivations.

Table 1.1 *Personal and tutor: dictionary definition and history*

Term	Definition	History
Personal	Adjective 1. one's own; individual; private	Late fourteenth century Middle English via Old French (twelfth century) from Latin *personalis* – 'as person'
Tutor	*Noun* a private teacher, esp. one in general charge of a person's education *Verb* 1. act as a tutor to 2. work as a tutor 3. restrain, discipline (*The Concise Oxford Dictionary*, 1995)	Late fourteenth century From Latin *tutor*– 'Guardian, Watcher' (noun) or *tutor* (verb) – 'to watch over'

As you can see, the modern word 'tutor' has a purely academic sense. However, the original Latin meaning of 'guardian, watcher' and its verb form 'watch over' is certainly relevant to the personal tutoring principles. Also, by putting the two together, with the adjective 'personal' modifying the noun 'tutor', we have a sense of a practice tailored to the individual. (The third definition of the verb 'to tutor' – 'to restrain, discipline' is something that we may relate to, if not directly in the support role!)

Table 1.2 *Coach: dictionary definition and history*

Term	Definition	History
Coach	*Noun* 1. an instructor or trainer in sport 2. a private tutor *Verb* 1. train or teach (a pupil, sports team etc.) as a coach 2. give hints to; prime with facts (*The Concise Oxford Dictionary*, 1995)	From the French *coche* (sixteenth century) as in *stagecoach*. Used in the athletic sense from 1861. Used as *instructor/trainer* from circa 1830 as a result of Oxford University slang for a tutor as one who 'carries a student through an exam'. (Online Etymology Dictionary, n.d., online)

Although there is partly an association with a particular field (sport), the term coach, both as a noun and a verb, contains meanings with immediate relevance: instructor, trainer, train, teach, give hints to. Its history gives us the highly relatable sense of 'carrying through'. A very pertinent image is provided with the meaning broadening from the literal physical carrying of 'stagecoach' to the metaphorical sense of carrying a learner through an exam. In our context, the 'carrying through' is widened to include many aspects of the learner from the programme of study and barriers to learning, to name but two.

The relationship between personal tutoring and coaching

You can see the common ground and also the subtle distinctions between these two terms. More often than not, definitions try to harness all of the component parts into what is usually quite a clunky and awkward sentence or series of sentences (but not our definition of the personal tutor... of course!). With this in mind, Table 1.3 provides our interpretation of the two elements divided into approach, core focus and context, along with how it helps learners. The jagged line illustrates the close relationship between the two.

Table 1.3 Relationship between personal tutoring and coaching

	Personal tutoring	**Coaching**
Approach	Can be directive (you take more of a lead and offer advice and guidance) and non-directive (encourage the learner to take more of the lead and reflect back the content they bring), focusing on stretching (intellectual/academic need) or nurturing (emotional need).	Can be directive or non-directive. Usually focuses on stretching (usually intellectual/academic need, but can be related to an emotional need if required).
Core focus	Following an educational/learning agenda. Develop longer-term trusting relationship.	Affect an immediate improvement in skills, approach or knowledge. Usually within short time frames.
Context	More relationship-based between the personal tutor and learner than a functional process.	More of a functional process, in other words designed to be immediately practical and useful.
How it helps learners	Helps learners acquire new skills and knowledge and nurture emotional well-being through regular communication, either through group tutorials and/or one-to-ones.	Helps to improve learner performance and skills through one-to-one coaching conversations.

Personal tutoring focuses on developing a trusting longer-term relationship with a learner through listening and regular communication. It can take the form of being directive and non-directive, focusing on working with individual learners over a significant period of time to advise and help them acquire new skills and improve their approach to learning – for example, developing their focus, motivation and skills in independent learning and reflection – as well as counselling them to nurture their emotional well-being and development.

Coaching skills and actions lend themselves more towards regular one-to-one conversations you have with learners either within a class, in the corridor or while having an arranged one-to-one meeting, in order to influence a more immediate improvement in performance and the development of skills.

To avoid confusing personal tutoring and coaching, we need to view them as related to each other but not the same. A personal tutor may include elements of coaching if the need arises, but a coach is not a personal tutor. Personal tutoring leans more towards being relationship based with the learner, while coaching is a more functional process to create an immediate improvement in learner performance.

Critical thinking activity 1

1. How well do the definitions of personal tutoring and coaching fit with your own experience, whether that is through 'doing', being on the receiving end or from observing these activities in practice?

2. From your own experience, how would you define personal tutoring and coaching? Make a note of your definitions so that you can see whether your definitions change as you read though the rest of the book.

As a trainee teacher, reading definitions of the two roles to develop your understanding of what a personal tutor is can be a good starting platform. However, let's now explore the definitions further and put the roles, as defined, into situations you can relate to.

CASE STUDY

Sarah's story

Sarah is a trainee teacher who is on her second teaching placement at a sixth-form college.

Week 1

Sarah has been given the job of meeting a large group of level 3 extended diploma business learners each week, on top of her teaching commitments. Her head of department has tasked her with delivering engaging group sessions focusing on CV writing, researching employers and universities as well as developing learners' employability skills. She must also work with each learner individually to review their individual learning plans (particularly focusing on assessing how each learner is progressing against their target grades) and to review and set new SMART (Specific, Measurable, Achievable, Realistic and Time-related) targets regularly. Her head of department has asked her if she could track and monitor the learners' progress throughout her placement and give feedback on their progress to the rest of the teaching team during the weekly departmental meeting. Sarah has found that she has been speaking to parents on the phone a lot when some learners have been late, absent or not meeting assignment deadlines. She has found this work challenging but rewarding.

Week 2

In her second week, while delivering an AS business studies class where the learners are working in groups to develop presentations, Sarah finds that she has time to work with learners individually to discuss their learning and progress. Paul, a learner in the class, confides in her that he is finding that he cannot keep up with all of the expectations of the course and he feels he is falling behind. It is obvious that he feels anxious. Sarah allows Paul to express his concerns and questions him to find out whether he is actually behind with his work and what reasons he believes there are for this. As the conversation develops, it becomes clear to Sarah that Paul isn't actually too far behind with his work but that his recent unexpected poor exam results have knocked his confidence. Sarah steers the conversation more towards Paul's strengths and enables him to explore the potential actions he could take to regain his confidence and get back on track. They agree some small next steps for Paul to take and decide to review the outcomes of Paul's actions in the class the following week.

Week 3

During her third week, Sarah has arranged to meet learners from her extended diploma group regularly for one-to-ones. She explores with each learner how they are feeling and encourages them to discuss what issues they are facing both within and outside the college. Sarah asks questions and challenges the learners to think about and express their issues a bit more deeply than they might normally, while providing encouragement and guidance if needed. Her main aim is to give the learners a chance to look at themselves more closely, to explore new ideas and help build their confidence. She encourages the learners to take the initiative, and any actions resulting from the meeting that contribute to their learning and progress remain their responsibility. She helps them to think about potential outcomes of the actions in more detail and how long they think it would take for them to show progress. Sarah has found working with her learners one-to-one is rewarding and a welcome change from normal classroom delivery. She has discovered that the learners tend to behave differently compared to when they are in a normal classroom or corridor setting and that for the remainder of the placement she is looking forward to this aspect of her role.

Critical thinking activity 2

» *Having read through this case study of interactions between a trainee teacher and learners, and drawing on your own knowledge and experience, decide which aspect of the role is being described in each instance – personal tutoring or coaching. Then compare your answers with those offered in the discussion below.*

Discussion

Week 1: more personal tutoring than coaching; Sarah worked on monitoring and developing the learners' academic performance and their employability skills, which will continue throughout her placement.

Week 2: more coaching than personal tutoring; through questioning and discussion Sarah helps Paul to explore the reasons behind his drop in academic performance and helps him to set his own actions and the dates to review.

Week 3: personal tutoring (however, there are strong elements of a coaching approach); Sarah starts to develop a long-term trusting relationship with the learners individually through regular communication to develop their emotional well-being as well as develop new knowledge and skills.

Other useful ways to understand the role of the personal tutor

Let's now try to unpick the role of the personal tutor and recognise the different types of help and support you can give to your learners. To do this, it will be useful to look at the diagram developed by Clutterbuck (1985) which should start to provide greater clarity. The diagram was designed to explore the role of the mentor in FE, but it is also a useful one to apply to the role and functions of the personal tutor.

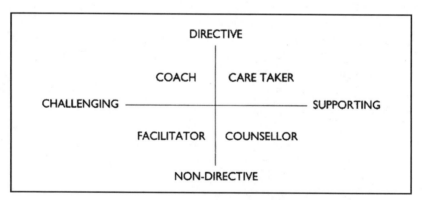

Figure 1.2 *Some ways in which mentors give support (Gravells and Wallace, 2007 (2nd edition))*

As a trainee teacher, your whole day is devoted to helping learners, but the help you provide can take many guises. Figure 1.3 provides typical personal tutoring examples related to Clutterbuck's 1985 model.

COACH (directive + challenging)

The directive actions you take with learners are where you actively attempt to help your learners to achieve a desired outcome and the challenging aspect is where you develop an intellectual need, for example to develop an improvement in a skill or in the learners approach to a problem.

For example, the coaching role could be where Sarah (trainee teacher) is observing a learners presentation, providing feedback and advice as to how they may improve it and setting improvement targets for the next time they present. It is worth nothing at this point that teaching, training and assessment (assessment for learning and assessment of learning) also appear within this section.

CARE TAKER (directive + supporting)

The supporting aspect of the model relates to helping a learner address an emotional need.

Therefore, the care taking part of Sarah's role might be where she takes a learner to learner services to make a referral for a service such as a meeting with a trained counsellor or an assessment for additional support.

FACILITATOR (non-directive + challenging)

The non-directive approach is helping a learner in response to a need that has arisen through a discussion or observation of a learner's circumstances.

The facilitator role could be where Sarah passes on names of colleagues within the institution who can offer possible career pathway advice or passing on contacts within local businesses who might be able to provide the learner with work experience opportunities.

COUNSELLOR (non-directive and supporting)

The counsellor aspect of helping learners usually relates to actively listening to them.

An example of this is where a learner may approach Sarah to discuss that they are being bullied. They may want to tell her how this is making them feel and discuss whether what they are doing about it is the right course of action. Sarah may ask questions to help the learner understand the situation more fully. More directive actions may happen at the end of this conversation to address the bullying issue.

Figure 1.3 *Personal tutoring examples related to Clutterbuck's 'some ways in which mentors give support' model (1985)*

As you can see, as a personal tutor you may be called upon to show an abundance of skills and perform a variety of roles within one lesson, group tutorial or one-to-one conversation.

To delve a bit deeper, let's put the above model under the microscope and look in more detail at the four main areas of helping learners (see Figure 1.4). In 2002, Klasen and Clutterbuck

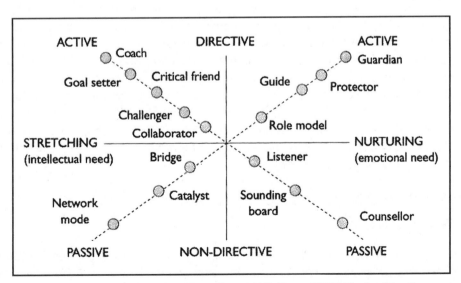

Figure 1.4 *Four basic styles of helping (Gravells and Wallace, 2007 (2nd edition))*

developed a more detailed model which helps us consider this further. Like Figure 1.2, this diagram was designed to explore the role of the mentor in FE, but we also find it useful to apply to the role and functions of the personal tutor.

Critical thinking activity 3

Take a detailed look at Figure 1.4: Klasen and Clutterbuck's (2002) model as adapted by Gravells and Wallace (2007).

1. Pick the two styles you feel you carry out the most in your current position (if you are yet to start teaching or your personal tutor role, from your own knowledge, choose which two you think you would do the most) and note down specific examples of when you have had to, or might have to, exhibit these styles of helping.

2. Using the examples you provided for question 1, list the qualities and attributes you:

    a. feel you displayed well which benefited the learner and the situation;

    b. feel you did less well and you feel you would like more opportunity to develop.

3. Note down specific next steps that you will take to start to improve the qualities and attributes you identified as needing development. Ensure you make your next steps SMART. They may be simple, small actions, for example talking to someone experienced who you have seen do these things well, practising them again with the same or a different set of learners, or asking someone to observe you and provide feedback.

Through varying degrees it is likely that you will exhibit all of the different styles of helping listed in Klasen and Clutterbuck's model and probably more within your teaching and personal tutoring career. As a teacher and personal tutor, both within and outside the classroom, you will switch between being directive and challenging (stretching) one minute to being non-directive and supportive (nurturing) the next. As your skills, knowledge and experience develop through constant practice and reflection, your ability to judge and even predict what approach you may need with learners will start to become less planned and more instinctively reactive, with you moving from being 'consciously incompetent' through to 'unconsciously competent'. However, you will not always get it right. The unpredictability of learner needs will always present new challenges and keep you on your toes. Nevertheless, this is part of the enjoyment of teaching and personal tutoring and one that will continue to challenge you throughout your career.

Which personal tutoring institutional model do you work within?

Imagine if an Ofsted inspector, or someone else with a vested interest, asked you: 'How is personal tutoring organised in your institution?' How would you answer? You may be new to the profession or the institution and not know; and there's no shame in admitting that. The question has a simpler version: who does the personal tutoring and who manages it?

Why is it important to know about models?

As we will see in the upcoming chapters, becoming outstanding means thinking critically about your role, its relationship to others in the institution and thus about the level of influence you may have. In order to do this, you will need clarity over your place in the institution along with knowledge of organisational structure and models. Armed with this knowledge, you can go on to see how your activities and objectives link to other levels of the institution, which will help you with personal development and promotional opportunities. As shown in the final chapter in particular, thinking about how you 'integrate vertically', in other words how your objectives meet the objectives of different layers ascending through your organisation, means employing the necessary critical thinking skills, both to be most effective in your role and to see beyond this immediate role. This is central to your career development.

Main personal tutoring institutional models

Generally, institutions organise their personal tutoring in one of the following ways.

Table 1.4 Main personal tutoring institutional models

Traditional	Centralised	Hybrid
Teaching staff have personal tutoring as part of their overall role and deliver tutorials and support.	A specialised and dedicated team of non-teaching staff (for example, 'super tutors') deliver tutorials and support.	A mixture of the traditional and centralised models.

Critical thinking activity 4

1. Thinking about the institution you work in, which personal tutoring institutional model is used?

2. What do you think the advantages and disadvantages of each are?

Discussion

Compare your answers with those suggested in Table 1.5 on the following pages.

Of course, we need to take into account differences that can exist within the particular institutional models themselves which may affect their relative effectiveness. For example, we have highlighted consistency as a key strength of the centralised model; however, if the 'super-tutors' are not directly line managed by learner support managers who direct and support them, along with overseeing the support structure, then inconsistency may still be an issue.

Table 1.5 *Advantages and disadvantages of different personal tutoring institutional models*

	Advantages			Disadvantages		
	For the learner	For the personal tutor	For the institution	For the learner	For the personal tutor	For the institution
Traditional	Learners may receive group tutorials and one-to-ones where curriculum topics are embedded more readily. This may be because a greater link with the curriculum area exists.	Personal tutors may have a greater overall knowledge of learners (since often their tutees are also learners whom they teach).	Departments may have greater autonomy in employing certain teachers as personal tutors for whom this is a strength.	Increased likelihood of learners having an inconsistent support experience as a result of inconsistent support processes (in part due to the number of staff delivering tutorials and support).	Increased likelihood of tutorial and support processes becoming secondary to curriculum. Examples include: • curriculum workload resulting in the personal tutor aspect of the teacher's role (for example tracking and monitoring) becoming neglected; • personal tutors using group tutorials and one-to-one conversations with learners as an extension of curriculum delivery.	Difficulties of communication and organisation between other staff (for example careers and those with responsibility for enrichment) and personal tutors (in part due to the number of staff delivering tutorials and support).

Centralised					
Learners are likely to have a more consistent support experience due to more consistent support processes. Specialised personal tutors are more likely to be, or become, experts in the diverse and wide range of knowledge and skills needed to support learners. Coaching approach more likely to be consistently applied.	The personal tutor is likely to be supported more strongly, both for day-to-day tasks and overall development. This support comes from peers (a 'close-knit', relatively small team of personal tutors) and support manager (depending on the structure of the centralised model).	Consistency of support processes: • effectiveness of tutorial and support structure and delivery is likely to be reviewed more often; • resources for support are likely to be more concentrated and reviewed more often; • avoids issues of tutorial and support becoming secondary to curriculum.	Unless strong communication links between personal tutors and curriculum staff exist, personal tutors' knowledge of learners' progress can be limited thus negatively impacting on the effectiveness of support that learners receive.	Can mean that curriculum staff view all personal issues, along with, possibly, behavioural and attendance issues, as 'someone else's problem' (in other words, the personal tutor's). If asked to deliver group tutorials to all learners, there may be resistance from 'super tutors' since this may be seen as more of a teacher activity.	There may be resistance from certain departments about what they see as an imposition of the centralised model at the expense of having the freedom to use teachers in personal tutoring roles as they see fit.

Hybrid

Will be a mix of the above advantages and disadvantages since it is a mix of these models.

General advantages:

- Since curriculum departments have different characteristics, some may suit the 'super tutor' role more than others. The hybrid model allows for certain areas to be targeted in this way.
- Curriculum areas may have more autonomy in deciding which support structure suits them.
- Comparison of performance between departments using different personal tutoring models to inform future decisions is made possible.

Summary

This chapter has introduced the personal tutor through definitions. It has explored the similarities and differences between personal tutoring and coaching and how outstanding personal tutoring encompasses these complementary principles. Whether you are an experienced teacher or a trainee, you will usually have to offer more to a learner's overall education and ultimate success than just traditional classroom teaching and this is where the outstanding personal tutoring principles can make the difference. Through examples and the two theoretical models in Figures 1.2 and 1.4, we have looked at the different types of support a personal tutor can give to learners.

Remember that developing the personal tutoring principles alongside your teaching skills will make you a more effective practitioner overall, which will positively impact upon your learners' progress and success.

We have also considered the advantages and disadvantages of different institutional personal tutoring models. In the following chapter we will delve into the core values and skills that make an outstanding personal tutor.

Learning checklist

Tick off each point when you feel confident you understand it.

☐ *I recognise that the principles of being an outstanding personal tutor are very similar, if not the same in most instances, as being an outstanding teacher.*

☐ *I appreciate that what 'success' ultimately looks like for each learner is very different because they all come from different backgrounds, have varying levels of skills and abilities, and each face different challenges throughout their learning both within and outside the classroom.*

☐ *I understand, as a teacher, that I am increasingly expected to offer more to learners' overall success than just teaching a good lesson.*

☐ *I recognise that there is a natural overlap between personal tutoring and coaching.*

☐ *I recognise that the key to becoming an outstanding personal tutor is regularly practising, and reflecting on the impact of, the personal tutoring principles.*

☐ *I understand what is meant by the three main institutional personal tutoring models (traditional, centralised and hybrid) and can evaluate them through their relative advantages and disadvantages.*

Critical reflections

1. To what extent do you believe your teacher training course and provider have focused on improving your personal tutoring practice?

2.   Analyse the importance that your current teaching or placement institution places on personal tutoring and explain how you have arrived at that judgement (if you have experience of more than one institution, using examples, compare and contrast two institutions' approaches to this).

3.   Discuss what impact you feel a significant improvement in personal tutoring practice could have on:

   a.   a learner's progress;

   b.   a department's performance;

   c.   an educational institution's performance.

4.   From your experience, compare and contrast the benefits and importance of traditional classroom teaching and personal tutoring.

Taking it further

Bullock, K and Wikely, F (2004) *Whose Learning? The Role of the Personal Tutor*. Berkshire: Open University Press.

European Mentoring and Coaching Council website (United Kingdom version): www.emccuk.org.

Gravells, J and Wallace, S (2007) *Mentoring in the Lifelong Learning sector* (2nd edition). Exeter: Learning Matters.

   The above title is useful in particular for discussions of the distinctions between mentoring, coaching and teaching (pp 10–11).

Gravells, J and Wallace, S (2013) *The A–Z Guide to Working in Further Education*. Northwich: Critical Publishing.

   The above title is useful in particular for discussions of coaching and mentoring (pp 27–31).

Neville, N (2007) *The Personal Tutor's Handbook*. Basingstoke: Palgrave Macmillan.

Whitmore, J (2002) *Coaching For Performance: Growing People, Performance and Purpose*. London: Nicholas Brealey Publishing.

Wootton, S (2013) *Personal Tutoring for the 21st Century*. Barnsley: Further Education Tutorial Network.

References

Clutterbuck, D (1985) cited in Gravells, J and Wallace, S (2007) *Mentoring in the Lifelong Learning sector* (2nd edition). Exeter: Learning Matters.

Confederation of British Industry, (2014) *Ofsted Consultation – Better Inspection for All*. [online] Available at: news.cbi.org.uk/news/ofsted-consultation-better-inspection-for-all/ [accessed May 2015].

Confederation of British Industry, (1995) *The Concise Oxford English Dictionary*. Oxford: Clarendon Press.

Howell, W S (1982) *The Empathic Communicator*. University of Minnesota: Wadsworth Publishing Company.

Klasen, N and Clutterbuck, D (2002) cited in Gravells, J and Wallace, S (2007) *Mentoring in the Lifelong Learning sector* (2nd edition). Exeter: Learning Matters.

Online Etymology Dictionary (n.d.) www.etymonline.com [online] Terms searched for: personal, tutor, coach [all accessed May 2015].

2 Core values and skills of the personal tutor

Chapter aims

This chapter helps you to:

- understand what the core values and skills of the outstanding personal tutor are and be able to distinguish between them;
- consider approaches to embedding the core values within your teaching and personal tutoring practice and apply them to different situations;
- develop techniques to improve your personal tutoring core skills and apply them to different situations.

Introduction

This chapter explores the core values and skills of the outstanding personal tutor in two separate sections through typical scenarios that you are likely to face.

Section 1: What are the core values of the outstanding personal tutor?

Now that you are familiar with the ways in which you can help learners, we look at the core values which should become increasingly evident in your day-to-day actions, behaviour and approach. This section doesn't aim to repeat your lessons on professional values and ethics, topics covered during teacher training under various guises depending on the educational institution. It does, however, sit closely alongside these topics to complement and reinforce some of the content you may cover and assessments you may undertake, as well as providing you with a more comprehensive learner support perspective.

The core values of the outstanding personal tutor are:

*   high expectations;

*   approachability;

*   diplomacy;

*   being non-judgemental;

*   compassion;

*   the 'equal partner, not superior' approach;

*   genuineness.

What is a core value and how do I know what mine are?

Embodying the core values of the personal tutor, when compared with other positive values, is fundamental to providing outstanding learner support. Furthermore, when they underpin the core skills (section 2 of this chapter) and key activities (Chapter 4), they can have a significant impact on learner outcomes.

So, what is a value and how does it relate to your personal tutor role? Values are things that you believe are important to the way that you live and work; and core values are those which hold the greatest amount of meaning to you. They are central to the decisions you make in college, the classroom and while working one-to-one with your learners. Another way to look at it is that your values are your guiding principles which shape your priorities and in many cases dictate your day-to-day behaviours and approach to people and work. Your values can be seen in the actions you take and in the way you respond to dilemmas, challenges and adversity. Halstead and Taylor (2000, p 50) define values as '*principles and fundamental convictions which act as general guides to behaviour, enduring beliefs about what is worthwhile, ideals for which one strives, standards by which particular beliefs and actions are judged to be good or desirable*'.

A core value is only truly a core value if you *live* by it and it can be seen in your actions (at least the majority of the time). When the things that you do and the way you behave match your core values, then you are likely to feel satisfied and content. For example, if you value working with people and you sit in front of a computer screen from 9am to 5pm every day, are you likely to be satisfied with your job? No. And that is because it is important for your core values and actions to align in order for you to feel that you are doing valuable work. At this point, it is useful to consider the reasons why you chose to pursue a career in education. Hang on to this thought as you read on.

Usually, values are perceived as quite abstract as well as difficult to identify and explain to others. When you discover your own core values, you discover what is truly important to you. A good way for you to try to understand your values is to think deeply about the following questions from a work-life and personal perspective.

Critical thinking activity 1

Identify examples of when you were the most happy, proud, fulfilled and satisfied at work.

1. Why did you feel that way?
2. What factors contributed to you feeling like that?
3. Now, try to encapsulate each of those examples into a descriptive word or words. For example, achievement, balance, generosity, happiness, mastery, self-reliance, teamwork.
4. Write these down in no particular order. Compare them as pairs and ask yourself: 'If I could satisfy only one of these regularly, which one would I choose?' Keep doing this until they are in order.

The words that you have listed could be seen as your individual core values. Identifying your core values isn't an easy task. When working with learners there can be many conflicting pressures and choices to make, and when many of the options seem reasonable it is reassuring to rely on your core values, as well as the values of the institution you work for, to guide you in the right direction.

How to develop the personal tutor core values

When was the last time you discussed your values or your department's values in a team meeting? It isn't normally something that comes top of a weekly meeting agenda, if it even makes it onto the list at all within an academic year. For you to understand the core values of the personal tutor, you need to see the values in action and the following case study and related activity allows you to do this.

CASE STUDY

Mark's story

Mark is in his second year of teaching sport within an FE college.

1. During a group tutorial with a group of level 2 learners studying sport, Mark sets a learning activity based around the emotive subjects of health, cancer and bereavement. One learner in the class becomes upset during the activity and in order to provide them with comfort, rather than just offering them an opportunity to sit this activity out, he suggests that he will get involved in the activity and they can work through it together, which the learner agrees to. Mark offers a number of personal experiences about the subject when they feedback to the class during the group session which the learners appear to appreciate.
2. Mark is delivering a lesson to a group of level 3 learners studying sport and exercise science, where, in order to achieve a distinction on their assignment, the learners

need to work in groups to show leadership by planning and delivering their own sports session to the rest of the class. A heated argument begins within a team where accusations arise that one of the learners is not trying and this is damaging the other learners' chances of getting distinctions. There are a number of options which Mark quickly considers, but he opts to mediate the situation. He speaks to learners on both sides of the argument to diffuse it, taking a non-directive approach, particularly using the question *why* repeatedly (this helps Mark to get to the crux of the issue because it digs deeper than just taking the first answer from a learner). Once he is clear about the issues from both sides, he develops consensus between the group members to be able to focus effectively on the task.

3. During an A level physical education lesson near the end of the academic year, Mark decides to set a mock exam paper under timed conditions which will be peer-assessed using the exam grading criteria. Instead of watching the learners take the test, he explains to the class that he will also sit the exam under the same conditions and put forward his paper to be assessed too.

Critical thinking activity 2

» *In each case decide which core value (from the personal tutor core values list at the start of this section) you believe Mark is embodying, and identify the positive benefit being created from this approach.*

Discussion

In the previous scenarios, Mark displayed the following core values of the personal tutor.

1. Compassion – this required Mark to put himself in the learner's position and to take action to ensure a positive outcome. Even though the action taken may not work with all learners, it does show that he understands their feelings and cares about their well-being. This also allows the learner to continue to engage in the learning activity.

2. Diplomacy – instead of Mark taking punitive action against the learners in terms of stating the possible negative outcomes of not engaging in the activity or suggesting disciplinary action, he showed good communication skills to sensitively and tactfully mediate the situation. Becoming skilled in the art of de-escalating a tense situation is a very useful way to be able to positively influence your learners.

3. The 'equal partner, not superior' approach – this is only one example, but there are many opportunities to display to learners that you understand what pressures they face and this approach also allows you to role model good behaviour and provide a positive attitude to stressful situations. Good parents try to instil positive core values into their children and as a personal tutor you can do the same when you role model your core values to your learners.

Let's now look at the remaining core values from the list.

Table 2.1 Remaining core values of the outstanding personal tutor

Core value	Explanation	Typical context
High expectations	To demand maximum effort and application from your learners.	The achievement of learners is closely linked to the expectations you place on them. Learners who are expected to learn more or perform better generally do so, while those held to lower expectations usually achieve less. Lowering expectations of learners can become a self-fulfilling prophecy, and the way to break this is to raise expectations for all areas of a learner's life and to ensure they receive the support they need to reach those high expectations. This will positively affect their grades and job prospects, as well as value-added scores and the success rates of the institution.
Approach-ability	The attribute of being seen as friendly, easy to talk to and discuss things with.	As you start to work with learners in one-to-ones, it can be obvious when something isn't quite right with them, either through verbal or non-verbal cues, for example lack of eye contact, negative body language and/or demeanour. Ways to appear more approachable to a learner in order to encourage them to be more open are to: • have friendly body language, in other words smile, do not sit with folded arms; • not be afraid to ask if everything is alright, using a general open question, for example, 'how are you?', 'how are things?'; • reiterate that they can trust you (obviously not to keep a secret if it might put them or someone else at risk of harm). You should realise this can take time; learners may not trust you straight away.
Being non-judgemental	Not viewing or labelling a learner as, for example, 'good' or 'bad'. In other words, you are making a conscious effort to avoid being critical of the actions of learners and trying to be open-minded.	It isn't easy to reserve judgement on a learner, and no practitioner (trainee or experienced) is entirely able to do so. However, the core value of being non-judgemental means striving to overcome the labelling of learners and always trying to give them the opportunity to show you their better side. It is important to say that, from experience, sometimes in this relationship you will get your heart broken. Some learners will not always rise to the challenge. However, if we go back to the principles of being an outstanding personal tutor, it is about motivating and inspiring them to achieve their potential. In order for a learner to achieve this and hopefully improve their behaviour or attitude, it is important to approach each of them with an open mind, as many times as you, the department or institution are able to do so.
Genuineness	Showing your true feelings and showing your learners that you truly care about their learning, progress and well-being.	As a general rule, learners are perceptive and can tell when a teacher is authentic in their concern for them. From experience, you will have greater success in helping learners to react in a more positive manner towards you if they feel that the help, advice and support you are providing is genuine and honest.

Individual and shared core values

Having established what the core values of the personal tutor are, you are hopefully thinking 'I believe I have a lot of these values (or similar ones) and I believe I show them through my actions a lot of the time when working with learners'. To really have an impact on learner support and, ultimately, learners achieving their potential, these values need to be shared and showed more consistently by other staff, as well as being recognised and promoted by middle and senior managers.

Core values directly affect employee actions, behaviour and organisational culture. Therefore, having positive, shared core values that everyone buys into (staff and learners) is one of the key ways to improve consistency of performance. An academic study (Guiso *et al.*, 2013) '*found that there is a relationship between a culture of strong values ("high integrity") as perceived by employees and organisational performance. That is to say, the values need to be "lived" throughout the organisation*' (The Great Place to Work Institute, 2014, p 5).

Learners' values

Alongside your own values and those shared within your institution, it is also worth bearing in mind the additional factor of the learners' values which can have an impact on your day-to-day work. As Carol Smith (2008) comments:

> it is equally important to be aware that the children we teach also have values and beliefs based on their social positions and experience, and that at some times these will be in agreement with the teacher's, but at other times they will conflict. ... Children's values are socially constructed and reflect their culture, family values and social influences of their local community. To include children fully in the school and classroom community, and to ensure positive learning experiences, teachers must understand the values children bring to school, and work with these to promote a positive attitude to learning, to themselves and to others, and encourage the valuing of diversity.
>
> (Smith, 2008, p 51; p 61)

Critical thinking activity 3

» *What three actions could you take to embed the core values of the personal tutor into your work with learners either within the classroom, in a group tutorial or working one to one?*

Discussion

Compare your answers to the following suggested ideas for embedding the core values of the personal tutor into your work with learners:

• explain the core values to your learners;

• display the core values on the walls of your classroom, with examples of actions that embody them;

- recognise and reward learners who display the core values of the personal tutor or other similar positive values;

- challenge negative values and allow that to be seen by other learners if appropriate;

- tell learners what they can expect from you (in other words, to display the core values);

- tell learners what you expect from them (in other words, for them to display the core values to you and their peers);

- try a learning activity in a group tutorial asking your learners to explain what the positive core values and associated behaviours are;

- relate values to learners' career aims by asking what are the core values of the profession they would like to enter.

Section 2: What are the core skills of the outstanding personal tutor?

Now that you have a firm grasp on how the outstanding personal tutor embodies the core values, let's look at the core skills. The core skills of the outstanding personal tutor are:

- building genuine rapport with your learners;

- active listening and questioning;

- challenging;

- reframing;

- reflecting back and summarising;

- teamwork;

- decision-making and problem-solving;

- role modelling;

- proactivity, creativity and innovation;

- working under pressure.

What is a core skill?

A skill refers to the ability to do something well. In addition, examples of synonyms for skill include expertise, adeptness, mastery, competence, efficiency, experience, professionalism, to name but a few. These highly descriptive words are connected with taking action or doing something, but also ensuring you do it well.

Core skills are the day-to-day actions you take to support your learners. Having the right skills is important to be able to carry out your job, but it is your core values that drive you to take those actions repeatedly. In essence, the core values lead and push you towards using your core skills. So, to have the greatest impact and to develop into an outstanding personal tutor, you need to have and use both the core values and skills together.

Different categories of personal tutor core skills

The core skills of the personal tutor can be broken down into different subgroups as seen in Figure 2.1.

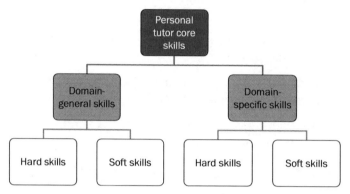

Figure 2.1 *Different categories of personal tutor core skills*

The first way to divide the core skills is into domain-general and domain-specific. Domain-general are common skills that may not necessarily be directly related to your personal tutor role and which you would find useful for most jobs, for example good communication, time management, problem-solving and organisational skills. Domain-specific skills are those that are more directly related to your personal tutor role.

Hard and soft skills

A further way to divide the core skills is into 'hard' and 'soft' skills. Table 2.2 gives examples of these.

Table 2.2 *Hard and soft skills examples*

Hard skills	Soft skills
Effective group tutorial and lesson planning.	Building rapport.
Developing a presentation or lesson resource.	Decision-making.
Effective one-to-one meetings with learners.	Reflecting back and summarising.
Helping a learner to develop their UCAS application.	Active listening and questioning.

Hard skills are normally related to a specific task or action, for example planning a group tutorial or undertaking a one-to-one, and we look at both of these in detail in Chapter 4. In terms of recruitment and selection, the hard skills are essential for getting the interview, but it is usually the soft skills (which are more personality driven) that will get you the job as educational institutions want practitioners who won't just perform their job role but will be a good fit within the department and make a good impression on learners.

How to develop the personal tutor core skills

We are going to focus on developing the core skills that we feel enable you to deliver outstanding personal tutoring. The following outlines an explanation and/or example of the personal tutor core skills.

Table 2.3 Core skills of the outstanding personal tutor

Core skills	Explanation and/or example
1. Building genuine rapport with your learners.	Developing a harmonious relationship with a learner in which each person is able to communicate effectively and understand the other's feeling or ideas.
2. Active listening and questioning.	Involves listening intently. It is important to be *seen* to be listening through verbal and non-verbal messages.
3. Challenging.	Using questions or statements to make learners think more carefully about their situation and challenge assumptions they may be making. This may help the learners to see things they may be failing to recognise.
4. Reframing.	Encouraging the learners to see themselves, others or issues from a different, or another person's, perspective. Often used in conjunction with challenging.
5. Reflecting back and summarising.	Showing the learners that you understand the content, feeling and meaning of what they have said through an extension of active listening. This is usually achieved through paraphrasing back to the learners what they have said.
6. Teamwork.	Working with fellow personal tutors to develop a tutorial scheme of work.
7. Decision-making and problem-solving.	Thinking through and making difficult decisions, even when there doesn't appear to be a clear consensus or solution.
8. Role modelling.	Showing your positive core values through the daily actions you take. This shows your learners what a good approach and behaviour looks like. This is where you 'walk the talk'.
9. Proactivity, creativity and innovation.	Trying out new ideas and approaches to constantly aim to improve your personal tutoring practice. In our experience, the most effective personal tutors are relentlessly proactive in seeking out and helping to address learner issues.
10. Working under pressure.	Staying calm in order to stay effective. Whether it is deadlines, competing demands, difficult situations or complex learner issues, this is something every practitioner grapples with at some time during the academic year.

You need to choose which of these core skills or which combinations of them are appropriate for particular contexts and learners. It is through practice and reflection that you will develop the experience to understand when one skill is more appropriate than another. The next two critical thinking activities explore two particular skills.

1. Building genuine rapport

Why is building rapport with people important? In short, if you have a strong, positive rapport with someone, they are more likely to understand and be responsive to your opinions and open to your influence.

Rapport between practitioners and learners positively influences learner enjoyment of their subject, attendance and time spent studying (Benson *et al.*, 2005). Additionally, rapport has been linked to increased learner attention (Buskist and Saville, 2004).

Starcher (2011) found that intentionally building genuine rapport with learners has positive consequences on their learning. For example, discussions flow more easily, student engagement (within and outside the classroom) increases, as well as their motivation for doing well on their course. In his research, he intentionally tried to build rapport with learners through one-to-one meetings and found that 95 per cent of the learners believed the one-to-one meetings were useful. He also reported that they felt more comfortable speaking out in class, asking him questions both inside and outside the classroom, and because of the one-to-one meetings they felt he was truly interested in them as individuals.

Building rapport with learners is something that comes naturally to some practitioners but takes more time and effort for others. The level of rapport is affected by your natural personality as well as the learner's nature and the context within which you work with them. For example, do you only ever see the learners in one class a week or do you see them more regularly in numerous classes, one-to-ones, group tutorials and enrichment activities? These factors can have an impact on the level of rapport you have. It is important to realise that the skill of building rapport can be learned and improved over time.

Critical thinking activity 4

» *Some techniques for building rapport with your learners follow. Think about them in general terms and from your own opinion and experience, rank the strategies one to seven, with one being the technique you view as the most effective and seven as the least effective. Also, are there any more techniques that you can add?*

Building rapport techniques	Rank 1–7
Making and maintaining sensitive eye contact	
Reinforcing and affirming the learner's gestures	
Subtly matching and mirroring body language	

Building rapport techniques	Rank 1–7
Varying the tone of your voice	
Picking up on favourite phrases or key words and subtly building these into the conversation	
Matching breathing rhythm	
Validating through active listening and asking open-ended questions	

Now that you have your personalised rank of techniques, start with number one and work through the list by practising and reflecting on the impact with your learners.

2. Decision-making and problem-solving

As you develop your career, you will realise that sometimes you can find yourself 'between a rock and a hard place'. There can sometimes be conflicting pressures, for example between doing what is right for the learner and what is good for the educational institution. Below are some potential scenarios you could find yourself in.

1. It is December and one of your level 3 learners on a vocational course wants to leave because he has found a job. The job offers reasonable training opportunities but it isn't particularly well paid and doesn't offer good promotional opportunities; however, he has said that he needs to start earning money. He is a capable learner and you expect him to complete the course with a good grade. In the last two academic years, the success rates on this level 3 course were deemed unsatisfactory by your head of department and the senior management at your college.

2. It is January and one of your level 2 vocational learners hasn't handed in a number of assignments to many of your colleagues for marking, but she has for your unit. She has relatively low attendance and poor punctuality, as well as displaying poor behaviour on occasion in other classes; but she works fine in your class. In your opinion, she is quite vulnerable and you believe she would struggle to get on another course or get a job if she left without achieving her qualification or progressing on to the next level. You are her personal tutor and have been trying to work with her through one-to-ones to improve her performance, but this appears to be getting worse. Most of your colleagues openly state that she should be removed from the course. The retention rates on this course have been very poor for the last three years.

3. It is February and one of your level 1 vocational learners has poor attendance; it is currently at 71 per cent and the institution's target for all learners is over 90 per cent. He has given you reasons such as illness and dentist appointments as well as family bereavements. You have been given a note on only a few occasions to explain these events. You are aware that he and his family have serious money issues because both parents are currently unemployed. The college asks you to

decide, based on progress at college, whether he should receive the weekly bursary entitlement money to help pay day-to-day living costs.

Critical thinking activity 5

1.   For each scenario, consider the following questions.

    a.   What decisions or actions would you take?

    b.   What factors would you need to consider?

As you hopefully appreciate, there isn't always a perfectly correct answer; there is only what is the best option for that context at that time. Doing what is right for the learner should be your first priority. However, this is easy to say. You may not be in a job very long if you always act against the institution! The ideal situation is when the institution always puts the learners' interests first through its shared values, policies and decisions. The institutional self-assessment system at the end of this chapter and those that follow illustrate ways in which 'bigger picture' issues can be influenced and prompt you to act.

Summary

The knowledge from this chapter sits alongside and complements your learning about professional values and ethics from your teacher training course. The core values of the outstanding personal tutor are your guiding principles which shape your priorities and, in many cases, dictate your day-to-day behaviours and approach to people and work. These principles are about putting your own agenda aside to focus on the best method(s) of supporting your learners. They can be seen in the actions you take with learners and can be shared by your colleagues, department and institution. When positive values are shared, this improves the organisational culture and ultimately the institution's key performance indicators.

Learning checklist

Tick off each point when you feel confident you understand it.

☐   *I understand that the outstanding personal tutor has particular core values and that it is important to take time to reflect on whether my current values and educational philosophy are consistent with my learners' best interests.*

☐   *I understand that core skills are the day-to-day actions I take to support my learners. Having the right skills is important to be able to carry out my job, but it is my core values which will drive me to take those actions consistently.*

☐   *I understand that hard skills are normally related to a specific task or action, for example writing a scheme of work or marking an assignment. Soft skills are more personality-driven: for example, active listening, building genuine rapport and questioning.*

☐   *I realise that all personal tutor core skills can be learnt and improved with practice and reflection.*

Critical reflections

1. Compare and contrast the similarities and differences between your own values as a teacher and the core values of the personal tutor.

2. To what extent do you believe your teacher training focused on improving your core skills? What, if anything, do you think could be done to improve this?

3. Evaluate whether outstanding hard skills or outstanding soft skills have the greatest impact upon learners' success.

4. How well do your colleagues display the core values of the personal tutor or similar positive values? What factors do you believe are influential in this?

5. To what extent does your current institution explain and promote its shared core values to its staff? If you have experience of more than one institution, compare and contrast the two institutions' approaches to its shared core values, using examples.

Personal tutor self-assessment system

What it is for

The personal tutor self-assessment system is designed for you and your institution to self-score current performance and identify targets for improvement against each of the book's chapter themes. You can use it to continually reflect and judge where you and your institution are against particular standards. You will achieve a score at the end of each chapter leading to a cumulative score at the end of the book. This final score will rate you and your institution separately as minimum standard, bronze, silver, gold or platinum.

Individual score and level boundaries	Institutional score and level boundaries
Minimum standard level = 0–19 points	Minimum standard level = 0–19 points
Bronze level = 20–39 points	Bronze level = 20–39 points
Silver level = 40–59 points	Silver level = 40–59 points
Gold level = 60–79 points	Gold level = 60–79 points
Platinum level = 80–100 points	Platinum level = 80–100 points

The self-assessment system is available as a free download from the publisher's website and the authors' websites (all listed at the start of the book).

How to use it

To identify current standards you should choose the level that best describes you and your educational institution. These can then be used to set targets for future development. Bear in mind when doing this that the levels are sequential and incremental. The content of the level below is not repeated and it is assumed this has already been achieved. For example, to achieve silver you will have achieved the minimum standard, bronze and silver content.

The personal tutor core values and skills are shown below to aid this chapter's self-assessment.

Core values:

- high expectations;
- approachability;
- diplomacy;
- being non-judgemental;
- compassion;
- the 'equal partner, not superior' approach;
- genuineness.

Core skills:

- building genuine rapport with your learners;
- active listening and questioning;
- challenging;
- reframing;
- reflecting back and summarising;
- teamwork;
- decision-making and problem-solving;
- role modelling;
- proactivity, creativity and innovation;
- working under pressure.

PERSONAL TUTOR SELF-ASSESSMENT SYSTEM: *Chapter 2 core values and skills of the personal tutor*

	Minimum standard 2 points	Bronze 4 points	Silver 6 points	Gold 8 points	Platinum 10 points
Individual (core values)	My day-to-day actions with learners generally display over half of the core values.	I am conscious to display all of the core values through my interactions with learners in lessons, group tutorials and one-to-ones.	I often reflect upon the impact that the core values have on the performance of my learners. The reflections inform my personal development targets.	The core values are reflected in the feedback I receive from observations of my lessons, group tutorials and one-to-ones.	I explain and promote the impact that the core values have on my learners, both within and outside my curriculum team.
Individual (core skills)	I regularly use over half of the core skills in lessons, group tutorials and one-to-ones, as well as with colleagues.	I use all of the core skills. They have a clear and positive impact on the relationships with my learners and colleagues.	I often reflect upon the impact that the core skills have on the performance of my learners. The reflections inform my personal development targets.	The core skills are reflected in the feedback I receive from observations of my lessons, group tutorials and one-to-ones.	I explain and promote the impact that the core skills have on my learners, both within and outside my curriculum team.
Institutional (core values)	My institution's values are similar to, or in some cases the same as, the core values. These are shared with new and existing staff at least twice within an academic year.	My line manager discusses the core values in team meetings. Discussions take place about how staff can embed these into their day-to-day activities, for example in schemes of work, lesson plans and one-to-ones.	All staff have a constructive appraisal which, in part, reviews how the core values are being embedded into every employee's activities.	All staff have a clear understanding of the core values and the importance of embedding them into their day-to-day work.	Learner voice feedback shows that the majority of learners feel the core values have a positive impact on their learning, progress and well-being.
Institutional (core skills)	Most staff use over half of the core skills with learners. Evidence of this is shown through learner voice feedback.	All staff receive regular training to develop the core skills and are encouraged to take ownership of this process.	Feedback from line managers routinely comments on employees' use of the core skills with learners and colleagues. This feedback informs the appraisal process.	The core skills are consistently and routinely improved through varied strategies. Staff are encouraged to implement ways of assessing how effective the core skills are at improving learner outcomes.	Learner voice feedback shows that the majority of learners feel that the core skills employed by staff benefit their learning, progress and well-being.

The self-assessment system is available as a free download from the publisher's website and the authors' websites (all listed at the start of the book).

Taking it further

Rice, L (2005) Promoting Positive Values, in Cole, M (ed.) *Professional Values and Practice: Meeting the Standards*. London: David Fulton.

Rosenthal, R and Jacobson, L (2003) *Pygmalion in the Classroom: Teacher Expectations and Pupils' Intellectual Development*. Carmarthen: Crown House Publishing.

Wilkins, C (2003) Teaching for Equality and Diversity: Putting Values into Practice, in Ostler, A (ed.) *Teachers, Human Rights and Diversity*. Stoke on Trent: Trentham Books.

References

Benson, A T, Cohen L A and Buskist, W (2005) cited in Wilson J H and Ryan, R G. Professor-Student Rapport Scale: Six Items Predict Student Outcomes, in *Teaching of Psychology*, 40 (2): 130–33.

Buskist, W and Saville B K (2004) in Perlman, B McCann, L I and McFadden, S H (eds.) cited in Wilson J H and Ryan, R G Professor-Student Rapport Scale: Six Items Predict Student Outcomes, in *Teaching of Psychology*, 40 (2): 130–33.

Halstead, J M and Taylor, M J (2000) cited in Smith C (2008) Demonstrating Positive Values, in Cole, M (ed.) *Professional Attribute and Practice: Meeting the QTS Standards* (4th edition). Oxon: Routledge.

Smith C (2008) Demonstrating Positive Values, in Cole, M (ed.) *Professional Attribute and Practice: Meeting the QTS Standards* (4th edition). Oxon: Routledge.

Starcher, K (2011) Intentionally Building Rapport with Students, in *College Teaching*, 59 (4): 162.

The Great Place to Work Institute (2014) *Organisational Values. Are They Worth the Bother? How Values Can Transform Your Business from Good to Great*. London: Great Place to Work Institute.

3 Setting boundaries

Chapter aims

This chapter helps you to:

- establish the necessary boundaries between yourself, as the personal tutor, and learners;

- establish the necessary boundaries between learners themselves;

- identify the following types of boundaries along with their rationale

  - expertise

  - temporal (time)

  - behavioural

  - peer;

- recognise and set boundaries with learners and clarify their purpose by examining boundaries in context.

Introduction

When you are carrying out support, with possibly much of it on a one-to-one level, you are nurturing individual learners and you can be closely involved with their emotional well-being. While this kind of support is undoubtedly what will make you most effective, it does come with a 'health warning'. It opens you up to the danger of getting 'too close' to the issues and by implication, at times, the learners themselves. Also, it can mean that your role feels as though it is crossing over into the realms of the social worker or counsellor. As one teacher said, '*I have three roles in my classroom: teacher, parent and social worker. Sometimes, the actual teaching part is the least important of all*' (*Guardian*, 2015, online). You may also be able to relate to this point from a head teacher, particularly if you have been in education for some time: *'We take away the barriers that are getting in the way of a child's learning. A lot of the social-work stuff has been absorbed into the school day.'* (Bloom, 2014, p 26).

The health warning is for both sides; in other words, for the good and protection of both the learner and yourself. On the learner side, recognising boundaries can avoid over-dependency when the aim is to provide comprehensive support but at the same time get the learner to take responsibility and to be independent. On your side, boundaries can help in looking after yourself and being able to compartmentalise the personal and professional, which can be crucial when faced with learners with varied, complex and challenging issues. It's also important to use opportunities to 'offload' in a constructive way with your colleagues. When this is done in a structured manner it is sometimes referred to in other fields, such as social work, as 'supervision'.

It is necessary for you to know where support begins and where it ends. This is not always easy to establish and there will sometimes be subtle judgements to make. The examples and case studies provided in this chapter aim to give you a picture of the subtlety needed. The chapter also explores the rationale behind the boundaries.

While there are obvious similarities to the topic of professional conduct in teacher training and CPD, the information here complements and sits closely alongside it as an exploration of the boundaries most relevant to the personal tutor.

In addition to the boundaries between yourself and learners, this chapter examines your role in getting learners to recognise boundaries between each other (peer boundaries).

What are boundaries?

You are probably already aware of the professional educational boundaries that you need to keep. Rather than covering all of them, in this chapter we look at the boundaries most relevant when providing a high level of individual, holistic support. In our experience, when excellent support which deals with underlying issues is given, it can sometimes raise further problems if certain boundaries are not recognised. It is these boundaries that we are concerned with here.

Boundaries can be best understood by grouping them into different types and by viewing examples hand in hand with their rationale (see Table 3.1).

Expertise boundaries

A research study into boundary dilemmas in teacher-student relationships concluded that *'there were times when our participants [teachers] struggled with the decision-making processes surrounding boundaries and recognised a significant lack of expertise in dealing with many issues their students faced'* (Aultman et al., 2009, p 645). Given this issue, you need to know when to recognise an expertise boundary.

Within your personal tutor role you may well feel you have to perform lots of other roles: for example counsellor, social worker or mental health worker. It is important to recognise that,

Table 3.1 Boundary types

Boundary type	Rationale	Examples
Expertise boundaries (Aultman et al., 2009, p 639)	You don't have the expertise or training; other people in your institution are employed for these purposes.	Mental health *Specific example:* A learner making suicide threats. Counselling *Specific example:* A learner who has suffered a bereavement. Safeguarding *Specific example:* A learner who you suspect may be the victim of sexual exploitation. Accommodation *Specific example:* A learner who has had to leave home and seeks advice from you about what to do.
Temporal (time) boundaries (Aultman et al., 2009, p 639)	You, as a resource for your learners, are not a limitless resource; equality and fairness to all of your learners needs maintaining.	*Specific example:* A learner with complex individual needs who could take up an increasing and excessive amount of your time.
Behavioural boundaries	Your responsibility is to *influence* learner behaviour, but you are not able to *control* learner behaviour; there is the structure of the disciplinary process behind you.	Poor learner behaviour *Specific examples:* Repeated 'low-level' disruptive behaviour from a learner over a period of time without any sign of improvement. A learner who displays violent behaviour.
Peer boundaries	The promotion of respect and professionalism among your learners.	A learner who does not recognise and apply boundaries with their peers *Specific example:* A learner disrespecting the views of a peer or peers through repeated mocking and what may be deemed 'bullying' (both verbal and through social media).

while you may employ skills which are common to those different roles, there is a line to be drawn between employing the skills and taking on the role itself. This is a judgement call on your part which is not always easy or clear to make. While this handover to others is necessary, it can be difficult for at least two reasons.

1.   More often than not, the learner is more trusting of you than any other member of staff, particularly those who have not been working with them through the course of an academic year to build a relationship. A young person who has had a traumatic experience or has a complicated background affecting the way they act is often unwilling to 'tell their story' again to another person, one who doesn't have the depth of relationship that you may have.

2.   It could be that specialist staff for these purposes may not actually be employed within your institution. As we mentioned at the outset of the book, these specialised services are unfortunately often the first to be cut as a result of budgetary constraints.

Temporal boundaries

One of the most enjoyable things about working with learners is that you don't know what will happen from one day to the next. While this can make the job a lot of fun, it also means it can be very difficult to predict how much time to spend on particular tasks, or, more accurately, working with particular learners. Once again, the line is not always easy to draw and relies on your professional judgement. A good line manager will give you guidance and help with this. The decision can lead to heartache and guilt – the feeling that you could do more and devote more time. It is crucial to recognise that the reason you can't always provide this support as fully as you'd like to is not down to individual failing but because you are a finite resource. The temporal (time) boundary, then, needs respecting for this reason, and also in order that you don't disadvantage your other learners whose need for support, on the face of it, may not seem so pressing. Moreover, it can avoid the trap of indulging learners' over-reliance on yourself rather than encouraging them to taking responsibility.

Behavioural boundaries

It is right that you challenge poor learner behaviour as much as possible and not avoid the issue by passing it on to others before addressing it sufficiently yourself. However, you need to remember that the structure of your institution's disciplinary process should be there for you when you have exhausted all individual measures to positively influence learner behaviour. Of course, your faith in the disciplinary process and support of the institution you work in is important and relevant here (see also Chapter 5). For now though, you need to recognise that you can only *influence and manage* learner behaviour not *control* it (using the word in a different sense to 'controlling' a class of course).

Acknowledging that there are boundaries to your own responsibility and authority in relation to learners' behaviour is a way of recognising that the time may come to refer the problem on. As shown in the examples in Table 3.1, this applies to both the repeated 'low-level' disruptive behaviour which continues over a period of time despite many interventions from yourself and the hopefully rarer instances of serious behaviour such as violence towards other learners or staff.

Peer boundaries

There is natural common ground between setting boundaries between you and learners and setting boundaries between learners themselves (peer boundaries). Here, there is clear overlap between setting boundaries and the ground rules of the classroom. Common examples include:

*   not talking over others;

*   listening and respecting others' views;

*   not being judgemental.

Good practice is for learners to identify these boundaries themselves in a group setting rather than being told what they are. This is always a good idea for a starter activity at the beginning of their course or when returning for their next year of study. On the matter of bullying, institutions should, of course, promote anti-bullying and have a clear policy and a procedure for learners to follow. A learner recognising bullying and having the confidence to disclose it, is itself something that may only come about because the topic is being addressed within group tutorials and reinforced in individual support. It is a good approach to encourage learners to make statements about specifics that have happened to them and to gather information from them about how they feel through a set of structured questions. Your support in enabling this is important. However, the next stage (the investigation) should be overseen by a manager. This could lead to a number of possible outcomes, including disciplinary action or the finding that bullying is not proven.

The young people you work with will all be at very different levels of awareness and application when it comes to relating to each other as peers and to respecting boundaries. This is where your support is so crucial. It is easy to fall into the trap of assuming that your learners know how to act towards each other as a given. Rather, you should acknowledge that they are likely to be at various stages of development in this area.

Critical thinking activity 1

»   *Think of a particular learner of yours who has difficulty acting appropriately towards his or her peers. Set three targets for the learner to develop recognition of peer boundaries.*

Discussion

Compare your answers to the following suggestions.

The following targets will be reviewed in two weeks' time:

*   *When other learners speak in class, listen to their point and let them finish without jumping in with your opinion.*

- *If a fellow learner has an opinion that you find strange, do not mock them or laugh at them, but ask them politely about it.*

- *Say 'I disagree with...' instead of putting down others by shouting out or using words like 'rubbish'.*

Using language the learners will understand (as in these targets) is all important if they are to adopt different behaviours. Equally important is a discussion, prior to the agreement of targets, about *why* these things are necessary. Learners' understanding of this makes it more likely they will actually act on it. Classroom activities can be useful to illustrate the targets; for example getting a learner to role play 'good' and 'bad' listening and then using peer and group discussion to explain the positives and negatives of these approaches.

The difficulty of letting go and when to do it

Letting go and handing over is necessary when you have exhausted all of your own supportive measures. The question is: how do you know when these really are exhausted?

Critical thinking activity 2

» *When did you last think that your own support of a learner had been exhausted? How did you know and what did you do about it?*

Discussion

You are likely to have found that the answer depends on the type of boundary. If it is 'expertise', it can be fairly straightforward to know when your level of knowledge, skill or experience is not enough. With 'behavioural', it could be when targets for improvement have been repeatedly agreed and not met; or it could be determined by the severity of the behaviour. With 'temporal' boundaries, your limit could be harder to pinpoint and it may rely on conversations with your line manager about time taken and on the judgement of yourself (as a finite resource) and your manager.

The issues shown in the final column of Table 3.1 are certainly ones that, generally speaking, negatively affect the key performance indicators you are charged with influencing: namely retention, success, attendance and punctuality, value-added and internal progression. Indeed, there is a tension between individual learner issues and institutional influences. You may find yourself in the middle of these competing pressures. However tempting it is to try and tackle such issues yourself, the boundaries we have been discussing need respecting for the good of all parties.

Boundaries in context

What does boundary setting and the recognition of boundaries with learners look like in practice? From the previous discussion it may seem that this mainly takes place at an individual level with learners, but one essential to good boundary setting is to write and agree a 'code of conduct' or 'agreement' with your learners in a group tutorial at the outset of the year. A good idea might be to get all learners to sign the agreement and display this on the classroom wall. It is important to distinguish such a document from the 'ground rules' of the classroom, although there is some overlap. Boundary agreements give you the chance to establish the different types of boundaries we have already discussed. For example, the specific time given to one-to-ones establishes a temporal boundary.

CASE STUDY

Jasmine's one-to-one with Asif

The following dialogue is an excerpt taken from a one-to-one meeting between Jasmine, a level 1 bakery learner, and her personal tutor Asif.

ASIF: *Hello Jasmine, how are you? Come in and have a seat. So, we've got your one-to-one today. We're going to talk about your attendance and how you're doing with completing your outstanding assignments in a bit. But first, we need to have a chat about the incident the other day in Tim's class...*

JASMINE: *You know why I do those things, I've told you a million times, I can't help it...*

ASIF: *Okay, okay, let's try not to get upset and have a calm talk about it. In a minute I'll ask you to tell me what happened from your point of view. First though, you're right, you have told me about things in your past that make you sometimes act in this way. However, our aim is to reduce these things happening.*

JASMINE: *Yeah but no one's had the difficulties I've had...*

ASIF: *Well, everyone does have individual difficulties and some people have had bad past experiences and that doesn't get in their way... we all feel different on different days, some days are good, some are bad... but on the bad ones we still act respectfully towards others.*

JASMINE: *But you get paid to be here.*

ASIF: *True [smiles] but your course is similar to a job in that you've agreed to the college rules by taking a place here just like we do when we take a job here...*

JASMINE: *Suppose so...*

ASIF: *It is true. Also remember the ground rules and boundaries agreement we agreed...*

Why don't you tell me what happened as you saw it... from your point of view?

JASMINE: *I just got dead wound up by him... the way he talked to me... and then when Jordan did that I flipped at her.*

ASIF: *Okay...*

JASMINE: *I know it was wrong, I shouldn't have done it...*

ASIF: *Why was it wrong do you think?*

JASMINE: *It just was... it's against in the college rules and that...*

ASIF: *Okay, well, it's good you've recognised that. But also the reason behind the rules is for everyone to feel safe and respected, and both Tim and Jordan didn't when you swore at them. Also, for when you leave college, it's to make you more employable, and that sort of behaviour just wouldn't be acceptable in a job.*

You realising it wasn't right was one of the things I was hoping for from this conversation. The other is to try to not repeat this again... because with the other incidents we've had already, I may have to refer you on to one of the managers to be part of formal disciplinary if we have any more. In that meeting, like this one, we want to support and understand you but the aim is to stop these incidents happening...

JASMINE: *I know, I know... I don't want there to be any more.*

ASIF: *That's good too. In terms of the difficulties you mentioned right at the beginning, remember I have been in contact with someone about your accommodation and I believe she's talked to you... how did that go?*

JASMINE: *Alright, we've sorted something.*

ASIF: *Good. And what about talking to someone else – Lyn, the counsellor – about the difficulties and feelings you have... like we mentioned last time you remember? ... had any more thoughts on that?*

JASMINE: *But I don't know those people, I only like talking to you because I know you... I don't want to talk to them.*

ASIF: *But I won't always be here... like if you go on to a different course next year... and they are specialists in this kind of thing. Talking about these things does help because it makes it clearer in your own mind and problems can seem smaller if you talk about them rather than when you just keep them in. Unfortunately, I just don't always have the time to talk through all these things for the length of time they deserve.*

JASMINE: *Suppose so.*

ASIF: *How about if I introduce you to Lyn myself and take you to her when you arrange a first meeting?*

JASMINE: *Dunno.*

ASIF: *Want to think about it and let me know by the end of today?*

JASMINE: *Yep, okay.*

ASIF: *Okay, good. I have another student who's been waiting for a bit. I'll type up what we've agreed and...*

Critical thinking activity 3

» *List which type of boundaries (from those listed in Table 3.1) are set or recognised by Asif and explain how he does this.*

Discussion

You may have thoughts about the relative pros and cons of how Asif conducted the one-to-one. This is useful and you should consider all such dialogues within the book in this way. Best one-to-one practice is itself a key topic within Chapter 4. So, for now, make boundaries your prime focus, while at the same time relating this generally to how the one-to-one was conducted.

Did you manage to identify which boundaries are established where and how this is done? Hopefully you will have seen that expertise, temporal, behavioural and peer boundaries are all recognised and conveyed to the learner in the exchange. You may have seen this in the following examples.

Expertise

And what about talking to someone else – Lyn, the counsellor – about the difficulties and feelings you have...

...and they are specialists in this kind of thing.

Temporal

Unfortunately I just don't always have the time to talk through all these things for the length of time they deserve.

I have another student who's been waiting for a bit.

Behavioural

...because with the other incidents we've had already, I may have to refer you on to one of the managers to be part of formal disciplinary if we have any more. In that meeting, like this one, we want to support and understand you, but the aim is to stop these incidents happening...

Peer

...the reason behind the rules is for everyone to feel safe and respected...

How does Asif get these across and is it grounded in the personal tutor core values of the Chapter 2? In the context of the conversation as a whole, and assuming appropriate tone and body language accompanies the words, I think we can say this is done supportively and exhibits the core values of approachability, compassion, being non-judgemental and being 'equal partner, not superior'.

There is always room for improvement of course and one observation to make is the amount Asif talks compared to Jasmine. More use of open questions could have elicited more from her. In place of '*remember the ground rules and boundaries agreement we agreed…*' consider it being phrased as the question, '*can you tell me some things from the ground rules and boundaries agreement we agreed?*' The latter gives Jasmine an opportunity to talk as well as checking if she actually remembers anything about these agreed boundaries.

Getting the learner to tell you the boundaries rather than the other way round and generally using active listening through open questions (more of which in Chapters 4 and 6) means the learner talks more in the meeting but, more importantly, takes greater ownership. The further steps are for the learner to take responsibility.

This is the key point and indeed is the overarching rationale for setting boundaries: for the learner to take responsibility and to be independent. As we have seen earlier in the chapter, it's easy for support to slip unnoticed into becoming 'doing everything for the learner'. However, the key purpose of good boundary setting is actually its opposite: for learners to be responsible for themselves and to be independent. Gomez *et al.* (2004, p 483) state that '*the caring work of teaching is premised upon having a reciprocal relationship between students and teachers*'. We need to remember this reciprocity and that it's a two-way relationship.

Summary

This chapter has demonstrated the importance of boundaries both for yourself and for your learners. Good boundary setting promotes the overall well-being and protection of both parties, with the central purpose of your learners becoming responsible and independent. It has defined the different types of boundary most relevant to the personal tutor along with specific examples and rationales. How this can actually be carried out in practice has been shown through boundary setting in an individual conversation with a learner.

Learning checklist

Tick off each point when you feel confident you understand it.

☐ *I understand the need for setting boundaries for the benefit and protection of both learners and myself.*

☐ *I understand the different types of boundaries most relevant to the personal tutor and the rationale for each: expertise – I need to use other 'experts' at times; temporal – I am a limited resource; behavioural – I can influence and manage but not control learner behaviour; peer – the promotion of respect and professionalism among my learners.*

☐ *I know how to set and recognise boundaries between myself and learners through an agreement and in individual conversations and meetings with them.*

☐ *I can see how effective boundary setting can enable learners to take responsibility and become more independent.*

Critical reflections

1. In your personal tutor role, to what extent do you believe you and your learners know and recognise the boundaries between you and them and between themselves as peers?

2. Can you think of particular learners of yours who you feel would benefit from having boundaries clarified to them? What boundary type(s) is it (are they)? How will you go about doing this?

3. To what extent do you feel your teacher training course has covered the boundaries examined in this chapter or similar boundaries?

4. How much emphasis does your current institution (and your colleagues within it) place on setting boundaries? What do you think could be done to improve this?

Personal tutor self-assessment system

The main boundary types are: expertise, temporal (time), behavioural and peer. See the following table.

Taking it further

Appleyard, K and Appleyard, N (2014) *The Professional Teacher in Further Education*. Northwich: Critical Publishing.

Department for Education (2011) *Teachers' Standards: Guidance for School Leaders, School Staff and Governing Bodies.* London: DFE.

Spenceley, L (2014) *Inclusion in Further Education*. Northwich: Critical Publishing.

References

Aultman, L P, Williams-Johnson, M R and Schutz, P A (2009) Boundary Dilemmas in Teacher-Student Relationships: Struggling with 'The Line.' *Teaching and Teacher Education*, 25 (5): 636–46.

Bloom, A (2014) Sometimes You Just Want to Cry. *Times Educational Supplement*, No. 5114: 24–8.

Gomez, M L, Allen, A and Clinton, K (2004) Cultural Models of Care in Teaching: A Case Study of One Pre-service Secondary Teacher. *Teaching and Teacher Education*, 20: 473–88.

Guardian (2015), *Secret Teacher: I Feel Like More of a Social Worker Than a Teacher.* [online] Available at: www.theguardian.com/teacher-network/2015/jan/10/secret-teacher-social-worker-emotional-students [accessed May 2015].

PERSONAL TUTOR SELF-ASSESSMENT SYSTEM: *Chapter 3 Setting boundaries*

	Minimum standard 2 points	Bronze 4 points	Silver 6 points	Gold 8 points	Platinum 10 points
Individual	I set boundaries between myself and learners and encourage peer boundaries at the outset of their course. These boundaries include expertise, temporal, behavioural and peer (phrased in accessible language for learners).	I revisit these boundaries in group tutorials. Through one-to-ones and other support meetings, learners have a clear idea of these key boundaries.	Through individual meetings, my learners are progressively becoming more able to recognise the boundaries. My learners are benefiting from clarity on a range of boundaries that help them to take responsibility and succeed.	My learners are becoming responsible and independent as a result of knowledge and application of boundaries.	Effective boundary setting is embedded in all of my interactions with my learners. As a result of this and other factors, my learners take responsibility and are independent.
Institutional	My institution ensures that all learners are given information on key boundaries to be kept between the personal tutor and learners and between learners themselves.	Managers give information to staff on how to set boundaries and provide resources for staff to use on this.	Departments or support functions review resources relating to setting boundaries. Line managers discuss boundary setting with staff individually for the purposes of learner and staff welfare.	Departments or support functions actively seek learners' views in boundary setting and integrate these into resources.	A range of different types of boundaries are set by departments or support functions which are informed by learners themselves. As a result of this and other factors, learners take responsibility and are independent.

The self-assessment system is available as a free download from the publisher's website and the authors' websites (all listed at the start of the book).

4 The learner experience: key activities

Chapter aims

This chapter helps you to:

- identify the key activities most relevant to your personal tutor role

  - ○ the tracking and monitoring of learners

  - ○ one-to-ones with learners

  - ○ group tutorial planning and teaching;

- identify the reasons for, and the benefits of, closely tracking and monitoring your learners;

- understand what at risk and vulnerable learners are and how to identify and allocate their level of risk;

- consider different methods of tracking and monitoring learner progress, including electronic systems; and identify appropriate supportive actions to reduce barriers to learning;

- examine strategies for conducting effective one-to-one tutorials;

- identify the reasons for, and the benefits of, group tutorials;

- examine good teaching principles and learning activities for group tutorials;

- explore appropriate group tutorial content for your learner cohort.

Introduction

In this chapter and the next we cover all of the things that a learner is likely to experience, either directly or indirectly, if they are given outstanding support. We give you a toolkit of actions to increase your learners' motivation for learning, as well as for them to aim to achieve above their targets. Furthermore, to help each learner to achieve these aims, we look at tracking and monitoring strategies that you can use to ensure that all of your learners have the necessary support from everyone involved, ranging from parents/guardians and outside agencies through to colleagues in your institution.

Strongly related to everything a learner will experience is the 'learner journey'. We have taken this term to mean a year in the life of a learner (in other words, in chronological order).

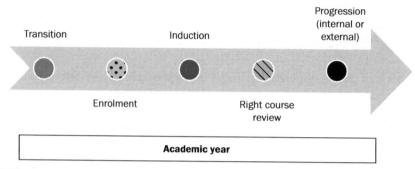

Figure 4.1 *The learner journey*

With the exception of enrolment and induction, the processes and phases within the learner journey shown in Figure 4.1 are discussed in Chapter 5. We don't examine these learner journey phases in chronological order; rather, we show you the personal tutoring tools, which cover all aspects of a learner's experience. The tools are illustrated through the key personal tutor activities:

- the tracking and monitoring of learners;
- one-to-ones with learners;
- group tutorial planning and teaching;

and the key procedures in chapter 5.

What is the purpose of the personal tutor key activities?

You will spend your time supporting learners in a variety of ways and settings. The main reason you track and monitor your learners, undertake one-to-ones and deliver group tutorials is to provide support so that each learner has the best chance of succeeding on their course and to help them successfully progress on to their next step. To do this you will be implementing individual actions to increase their motivation, remove or reduce as many of their barriers to learning as possible as well as, for example, to develop their employability skills.

All of the activities and strategies within this chapter are designed to achieve good standards of attendance, behaviour and completion of work ('ABC'). Achieving high standards of ABC helps your institution achieve one of its aims: strong key performance indicator measures relating to retention, success, attendance and punctuality, value-added and internal progression, as well as helping your institution to show its progress when Ofsted visit.

The tracking and monitoring of learners

Key activities to improve the success of your learners are:

* to regularly track and monitor the progress of every learner in your cohort, with a strong focus on at risk and vulnerable learners, taking into account the views of all of the staff who work closely with them;

* to provide each learner with accurate and regular feedback about how they are progressing and to agree SMART targets stating what they need to do to improve.

What do we mean by at risk and vulnerable learners?

In 1983, an article entitled 'A Nation At Risk' published by the National Commission on Excellence in Education used the term 'at risk'. So the term has been around for over 30 years. During that time, however, it has taken on a more specific meaning. Within educational institutions, the term is sometimes used interchangeably with 'vulnerable'. We have made the subtle distinction as follows:

* at risk – the extent to which learners are 'at risk' of not passing their study programme/qualification/course or under-achievement against target grades (see Table 4.1 for further detail);

* vulnerable learner – similar and interlinked with 'at risk'. The extent to which learners are vulnerable is determined by their circumstances or background, which may have the potential to impact negatively on attendance, behaviour or completion of their course.

What characteristics might mean a learner is at risk or vulnerable?

Some of your learners may have background characteristics (either from their past or which develop during their time in the institution) which may increase the chances of them being at risk or vulnerable.

So, how might you identify whether your learners could be deemed at risk or vulnerable? The following characteristics are not exhaustive. To enable you to think more broadly about where these influences may stem from we have grouped them under the headings of learner, family and society. We have used a Venn diagram to show how these groupings are closely interlinked and how any given at risk/vulnerable learner can be within one, two or all three groupings (see Table 4.1 and Figure 4.2).

Table 4.1 *Characteristics of at risk or vulnerable learners.*

Learner	Family	Society
The learner has: • a history of safeguarding issues, academic failure and/or suspension or exclusion; • a history of alcohol and/or substance misuse; • an identified learning difficulty; • emotional and/or behavioural issues; • English as a second or other language; • frequent interaction with low-achieving peers, for example involvement in gangs.	The learner: • is living independently; • has a history of abusive relationships or domestic violence within the family; • is in care or is a care leaver; • has a history of homelessness; • is receiving benefits; • is receiving disability living allowance; • is a teenage parent.	The learner: • is an unaccompanied asylum seeker; • has displayed offending behaviour and/or has had contact with the police or justice system; • has been previously identified as being at risk or vulnerable by a former educational institution or local authority.

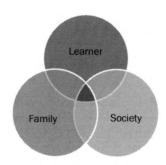

Figure 4.2 *Groupings of at risk/ vulnerable characteristics*

Just because learners may have one or more of the background characteristics listed that does not mean this will necessarily have a negative impact on their progress. Likewise, it is important to remember that you may have learners who don't have any of the characteristics listed and yet they still do not complete their course. However, it is good practice to consider these factors when deciding whether to designate the learner as being at risk and to inform at-risk meetings (discussed later in this chapter).

The tools to keep your learners on track to succeed

This section aims to provide a good practice model for learner tracking and monitoring. You may not recognise some of the terms used in the Table 4.2 – for example 'staff comments about learners', 'cause for concerns or congratulations' – as these differ depending on the institution you work for. However, even though the terms may differ, the meaning behind them is usually the same, whichever learner you work with or institution you work for. Table 4.2 outlines some of the key activities you can use to ensure learners succeed.

Table 4.2 *Tracking and monitoring activities*

Method	Explanation
At-risk meetings	• Formal meetings where you discuss the progress of each of the learners in your cohort in turn. • Discussion focuses on each learner's progress in relation to ABC and SMART targets. • Discussion takes place with other teachers and support staff who work with those learners.
At risk categorisation	• Where you identify the likelihood that learners may not pass the course or achieve their target grade. • You will take a holistic view of each learner's progress and profile. • Remember, your role is to improve the intellectual and academic ability and nurture the emotional well-being of your learners. These factors can influence the learner at risk category (discussed in detail later in this chapter).
At risk documentation	• Methods by which you record the reasons for your learners' at risk categories. • At risk documents should be seen as 'live', in other words they should be added to and updated accordingly over the academic year. • The method for recording isn't as important as actually going through the process of identifying the at risk category and support needs of every learner with the relevant teachers, support staff and managers. • It is good practice for you to notify all staff who work with a learner on a regular basis of the learner's at risk category, reasons for this and supportive interventions. This establishes a more informed and co-ordinated approach to each learner's individual needs.
One-to-ones with learners	• Arranged and structured conversations that allow you to discuss the progress the learner is making. • Where SMART targets are agreed along with actions for improvement and dates when these will be reviewed.
Course progress feedback	• This can be discussed with the learner within the classroom or in a one-to-one situation. • How well (or not) learners are doing on their course will affect their at risk category, indicating for example that they are at risk of not achieving the C part of ABC (completion of work).

Table 4.2 (cont.)

Method	Explanation
Parental contact	• It is likely that you will not receive all of the information you need to inform your decision to place a learner in a particular at risk category from your fellow colleagues and the learner themselves. For instance, for a number of reasons, learners may not always inform you of what is happening in their lives outside of the institution. • Regular parental contact is another method to inform the holistic view you must take to develop an accurate at risk category and to gain buy-in and support from them for the actions you are taking to support their son or daughter. • '...parental involvement plays a critical role in a student's education decisions. Students whose parents are involved in their education are more motivated academically, attend school more consistently, perform better in school, behave better...' (The Education and Economic Development Coordinating Council At-Risk Student Committee, n.d., p 2).
Staff comments about learners	• The majority of institutions now have an electronic system for monitoring individual learner progress. • Usually these systems allow teachers and support staff to make comments (positive or negative) about every learner's progress. • This information is usually visible to all staff (and learners and parents/guardians in some institutions) and is vital to inform the at risk category and supportive actions.
Cause for concern or cause for congratulations	• Electronic learner tracking and monitoring systems usually allow staff to share when learners are causing real concern or when they have really excelled. • These things need to be recognised and sometimes discussed with the learners and will partly inform their at risk category and the supportive actions you will take.

Critical thinking activity 1

1. In relation to the tracking and monitoring activities in Table 4.2:

    a. How many of these have you explored during your teacher training or on subsequent CPD courses?

    b. How many of these have you discussed with your own tutor, mentor and/or line manager?

    c. How many of these have you used in your practice as a personal tutor?

2. Rank the eight activities listed in Table 4.2 in order of what you feel has the greatest impact on your ability to track and monitor whether all of your learners are on track to succeed (1 = greatest impact).

3. The eight activities listed are only *some* examples of tracking and monitoring activities. What others can you think of?

Feedback to the learner

To be truly effective, all tracking and monitoring activities must inform timely and effective feedback to the learner. To achieve this, depending on the time you are given within the institution, the aim is to have regular discussions with every learner in your cohort to convey how they are progressing against their SMART targets. Discussions can take place at any time, whether that is in the classroom or corridor, on the phone, in a one-to-one or at a parents' evening. However, usually the most effective method is through an arranged one to one.

For learner feedback to be effective it must:

• be a two-way conversation in which, where appropriate, you employ many of the core skills discussed in Chapter 2; for example, active listening and questioning, challenging, reframing and reflecting back, and summarising;

• involve the learner doing the majority of the thinking and talking. Ineffective feedback is where you do the majority of the talking and the learner is passive. You should be trying to get the learners to think and reflect about their own progress and develop agreed targets with you.

Critical thinking activity 2

» *Think of the most useful face-to-face feedback you have ever had which you acted upon and which helped you to improve. List the factors which made that feedback so effective.*

How risk is assigned to a learner

When you start to work with your learners within the classroom, through group tutorials and one-to-ones, you will be creating a picture in your mind of the type and level of support each will need in order to be successful on their course. Regularly speaking to colleagues and using the institution's electronic learner tracking and monitoring system are equally of importance to inform your view of each learner's progress. So that you and everyone who works with the individual learners are clear about the support they need, it is useful to assign an 'at risk' category to each of them.

The at risk category helps you and other colleagues to have a clear overview of your cohort and to decide the actions needed to support each learner effectively. As the academic year progresses and each learner's situation changes, so should their at risk status and the level and type of support you provide. It is good practice to review each learner through formal at-risk meetings at regular intervals to ensure that you are tracking and monitoring that each is on course to succeed. Table 4.3 illustrates suggested at risk categories and criteria by which learners can be categorised.

Table 4.3 *At risk categories and criteria*

| At risk category | Criteria | | | | |
	Progress against SMART targets, including target grades	Attendance and punctuality	Behaviour/ disciplinary issues	Effort	Background characteristics
Outstanding	The learner is making exceptional progress above their SMART targets and target grade.	100%			
No risk					
Medium risk					
High risk					

Critical thinking activity 3

1. Table 4.3 provides general at risk categories along with the main criteria that determine them. Thinking about your institution, complete the table with phrases or statistics that describe particular features for each at risk category under each criterion. An example of a phrase and a statistic is provided in italics for you.

2. Pick one of your current personal tutor groups and allocate each learner an at risk category based on a holistic view of their progress so far. Then:

    a. calculate the percentage of learners who fall into each category currently;

    b. estimate the percentage you would like in the outstanding or no risk category by the end of the course/academic year.

Discussion

The reason we have asked you to provide your own specific criteria is because each institution is different and therefore will have different conceptions of what puts a particular learner at a particular level of risk. For example, one institution may consider that a learner who has below 85 per cent attendance is at high risk, but another may only consider that learner to be at medium risk. Also, it is important to note that institutions may have created their own at risk categories with associated criteria (different to those shown in Table 4.3) and indeed they may use a different term for 'at risk'. Therefore, it will be useful for you to ascertain, if you don't know it already, what terminology is used in your own institution and what definitions are provided.

Another aspect that you should consider is how at risk categories are used. Are they to be used to simply reflect whether learners will pass or fail their course or should they incorporate a more holistic view (for example, including background characteristics)? In this chapter, we are proposing the holistic view because personal issues are strongly linked to a learner's success. However, senior managers may only want to use it to reflect whether learners will pass or fail their course, and you may find it useful to reflect on why this might be.

A final point to consider is, to what extent should you share the categories with the learner and or parent/guardians? Although institutions may use this categorisation primarily for their own purposes, arguably it is useful for learners to be aware of their at risk status for motivational purposes. Similarly, parents or guardians may find this a useful indicator of their child's progress.

At risk meetings

Once an at risk category has been assigned to each of your learners, it is important to regularly review the reasons for the at risk category and the actions being taken to support every learner. Where regular at-risk meetings are a requirement or are common practice, they are usually most effective when they are:

*   undertaken on a regular cycle;

*   run as formal meetings in which anecdotal comments, gossip and any 'moans' are kept to an absolute minimum;

- attended by staff who work closely with the learners in question, including teachers, support staff and managers where appropriate.

If at-risk meetings are not a requirement, or common practice, at your institution, then an alternative strategy that you could adopt might be to regularly have informal discussions with your colleagues about learners who are deemed *most* at risk. The purpose of these discussions should be to evaluate the impact of current supportive actions and to agree future actions.

Within formal at-risk meetings, your role as personal tutor is to lead the conversation and discuss each learner in turn to review the reasons for their at risk category, what actions have been, and need to be, taken to support that learner to be successful (in other words, to keep them at, or move them towards, being no risk or outstanding), with dates when these actions will be reviewed. It is important to remember that this method of tracking and monitoring is not solely focused on learners who may be at risk of failing or withdrawing from their course; it should be equally focused on learners who may be at risk of not achieving their target grades. The former helps to improve retention and success rates whereas the latter helps to improve value-added scores. Together, they improve the overall learner experience.

The name given to at-risk meetings will differ between institutions and some may not have them at all. If this is the case, it is not your role to formally implement this system. However, it would be a relevant institutional aim to do so because experience suggests that this is a good practice model and gets positive results both for the learners and the institution.

Critical thinking activity 4

» *Table 4.4 is an excerpt from a live at risk monitoring document. This is an overview of learners with the at risk category for each, which includes reasons for the category and support actions taken. It is completed by you as personal tutor and is an example of at risk documentation as mentioned in Table 4.2. Read the document and write down what actions you would take to support these learners.*

Table 4.4 *Example at risk monitoring document (excerpt; actions omitted)*

Learner name	At risk category	Reasons for the category
Thomas Barber	High risk	Thomas displays a poor attitude to learning and is at risk of not achieving his target grade, as well as potentially being withdrawn from his course due to non-submission of work. He struggles with his written expression but is very good in presentations and class discussions when he focuses. He regularly displays poor behaviour and distracts others in the group. He has had a number of positive learning conversations [covered in detail in the Chapter 5] and is being taken through the formal disciplinary procedure. He has a number of safeguarding concerns due to his home life. However, there isn't much detail available in his safeguarding file.

Table 4.4 (cont.)

Learner name	At risk category	Reasons for the category
Laura Fellows	Outstanding	Laura displays an excellent attitude to learning and has excellent attendance and punctuality. She is working at her target grade level. However, she does want to achieve higher than this for her preferred university course.
Qasim Mohammed	Medium risk	Qasim is at risk of not achieving his target grade. He started the course enthusiastically and did very well for all of his assignments in the first few months. Recently, he appears to have lost interest in his studies. He had good attendance and punctuality; however, this has now started to fall. He works a lot of evenings.
Rachael Ward	High risk	Rachael is a young carer for her ill mum. She suffers from anxiety, which can lead to panic attacks in class. She is academically able and motivated; however, she has fallen behind with her assignments. Her target grade is distinction, but due to poorly presented work as well as some non-submission of assignments she is currently only achieving passes. Attendance is currently 68 per cent, with poor punctuality.

Discussion

When documenting the support actions for learners, it is important to:

- keep previous actions on the at risk document as you progress through the academic year. This helps to show any progress and also gives a clear overview of the support given to each learner;

- ensure that your actions to support the learner include, for example, parental contact and meetings, one-to-ones and SMART targets. Supportive actions should not be, for example, transferring or withdrawing the learner from the course. These would be the final result, not the supportive actions taken;

- share this information with as many colleagues who will be supporting that learner within your institution as possible; for example teachers, support staff and managers. Ensure that anything sensitive or confidential is not mentioned within a document like this. However, it is acceptable to note, for example, that a learner has a safeguarding file and who colleagues can speak to in order to find out further information.

Critical thinking activity 5

» *Using the group you identified in Critical thinking activity 3, complete an at risk monitoring document that includes all of your learners. State the at risk category, reasons for assigning learners that status, actions taken so far to support each learner and future actions you will take.*

Electronic learner tracking and monitoring systems

Electronic learner tracking and monitoring systems are the norm in the majority of educational institutions. There are numerous companies in the marketplace that offer systems which broadly do a similar job. In this section we are not going to name all of the different systems or list their characteristics. However, we feel it is important to illustrate some of the most useful features for achieving the best outcomes for learners.

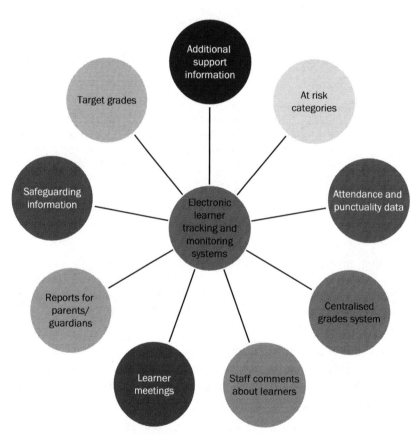

Figure 4.3 *Useful features of electronic learner tracking and monitoring systems*

Overall, the most important element of these electronic systems is that they are a 'one stop shop' for all information about every learner. Information about individual learners or whole classes should be updated by all teachers and support staff and is visible in real-time. These attributes are what make these systems so useful to your personal tutor role and key activities.

Table 4.5 *Useful features of electronic learner tracking and monitoring systems*

Feature	Why it is useful
Additional support information	Learners with additional support needs should have their support requirements available instantly, enabling more informed lesson planning and decision making by teachers, personal tutors and support staff.
At risk categories	Allows all staff to instantly see all learners' at risk categories. This enables quicker decisions to be made about support requirements and allocation of resources.
Attendance and punctuality data	Enables you and other staff to identify any issues or any patterns which will inform learner and parent meetings, one-to-ones and inform SMART targets.
Centralised grades system	Provides a clear overview about a learner's or class's academic progress. This is particularly useful in one-to-ones to inform SMART target setting.
Staff comments about learners	Provides instant feedback from any member of staff about a learner, particularly his or her progress against attendance, behaviour and completion of work standards. This qualitative information is useful in one-to-ones, when making parental contact and in disciplinary meetings.
Learner meetings	These meetings with learners are useful for documenting progress against SMART targets. It also allows you to document and share discussions you have had (with learners) with all colleagues to inform support.
Reports for parents/ guardians	Parental/guardian support and buy-in is vital when you are trying to help learners succeed. Instant access to these reports gives you a snapshot of every learner's progress at key points in the academic year and this enables you to use positive comments and constructive criticism to inform the decision over at risk category and one-to-one meetings.
Safeguarding information	Due to confidentiality it is unlikely to include any specific issues, rather, it acts as a 'flagging up' that a safeguarding file for a particular learner is held and that staff can see the designated safeguarding officer for more information, if required. This section is vital for keeping every learner safe. The previous 'staff comments about learners' feature provides a good overview of the progress of every learner, which, when twinned with safeguarding information clearly informs the at risk category, supportive actions and learner meetings.
Target grades	Enables you to set and review effective SMART targets in order to help bring learners up to their target grade or stretch and challenge them to achieve higher.

Good practice tips when using electronic learner tracking and monitoring systems

- Ensure you use clear language which the learners and staff can understand, and avoid misinterpretation. This includes being clear about why you are putting information on the system. For example, if you include a comment that the learner is having a difficult time, clarify that you are putting this on the system because you want other personal tutors, teachers and support staff to be sensitive around the learner at this time.

- Always use SMART targets where applicable.

- Ensure updating of information about learners is done in a timely manner, particularly in relation to the features shown in Figure 4.3.

- It is good practice to address the learner in reports to parents/guardians.

- In reports to parents/guardians, and where comments can be made about a learner within your electronic system, try to not be *overly* critical of the learner. In other words, try to turn a negative point into a positive action that could be taken by the learner. For example, try not to say, 'Sarah doesn't take part in lessons'; instead, say, 'We have agreed a target for Sarah to contribute to lessons every day'. This provides clear instruction on how improvements can be made.

Critical thinking activity 6

1. With every learner tracking and monitoring system, whether electronic or not, there can be problems or issues. Identify:

    a. what you think these are most likely to be;

    b. what actions you or the institution could take to overcome them.

2. If you are a trainee teacher and are not permitted access to the electronic learner tracking and monitoring system, but are responsible for tutoring learners, what issues does this raise?

One-to-ones with learners

Following on from tracking and monitoring, one-to-ones with learners is the second personal tutor key activity that we explore.

John Crace states:

> the [one-to-one] tutorial has been an integral part of the learning and monitoring process at many colleges – a forum where both teachers and students can discuss progress and set targets – and there is a great deal of evidence to indicate that it has played a key role in raising standards and student retention.
>
> (Crace, 2002, online)

CASE STUDY

One-to-one meeting between Anne and Chloe

The following dialogue is taken from an arranged one-to-one meeting between Chloe, an A level learner, and her personal tutor Anne.

ANNE: *Come in and sit down Chloe.*

CHLOE: *Thanks.*

[Anne is sitting at a table with her back to the door. Chloe sits in the only chair available at the other end of the table.]

ANNE: *Are you good?*

CHLOE: *Er... yeah, I guess so.*

ANNE: *Good! So are you getting on okay with your studies?*

CHLOE: *...Erm, I'm okay I think. I'm not sure... I'm trying my best to get all of the work done but I've had so much to do lately... I've been struggling a bit to get all of my homework and coursework in on time.*

ANNE: *You've been struggling? ... What's gone wrong?*

CHLOE: *Nothing's gone wrong as such... I've just had a lot on with my English coursework and revising for the mock exams... I've also been having some problems at home.*

[Anne turns her back to Chloe to face her computer]

ANNE: *Hang on, I need to make sure I get all of this down onto the one-to-one part of our system.*

CHLOE: *Okay.*

ANNE: *So, just say again, what's gone wrong?*

CHLOE: *Erm... I'm doing okay, but I've felt like I've been getting a bit behind with my work.*

ANNE: *Okay, do you remember your targets from our last one-to-one meeting?*

CHLOE: *I think it was to revise for my biology mock exam, complete my English coursework and... something else, I can't remember.*

ANNE: *I can't either. I'll check in a minute. What other A levels do you do?*

CHLOE: *History.*

ANNE: *Oh yes, I remember. So, did you revise for your biology mock exam?*

CHLOE: *I tried to get as much done as possible at home, but it wasn't easy... I did much better than I thought I would though. I was really pleased, I got a B!*

ANNE: *Right. Did you get your English coursework in as well?*

CHLOE: *It was late, but yes.*

ANNE: *Good... I can also see that you've had a few causes for concern from your history teacher, Matt. Tell me what you did wrong.*

CHLOE: *Nothing, I haven't done anything wrong... I had to have some time off because of the problems I've had with my stepmum.*

ANNE: *Okay, did you see Matt about this though? Because you need to tell him if you're going to be off.*

CHLOE: *No, I didn't, sorry.*

ANNE: *Well you need to make sure you do next time... we're not mind readers! You have to tell us if you've got a problem.*

So, the targets I want you to achieve by the next time we meet are full attendance, no causes for concern from your teachers and make sure you get all of your work in on time. Okay?

CHLOE: *Alright.*

ANNE: *Okay, great! I've got an important meeting I need to get to now, so I'll let you know when our next one-to-one meeting is. Okay?*

CHLOE: *Yes... fine.*

Critical thinking activity 7

»   *How would you evaluate this meeting? Note down three points about the meeting which you feel would make useful areas for development for Anne.*

CASE STUDY

One-to-one meeting between Anne and Chloe — take two

ANNE: *Come in and sit down Chloe, it's nice to see you.*

CHLOE: *Thank you.*

[Anne is sitting near Chloe, partly facing her at an angle; in other words, not sitting directly facing her. There is no table between them and Anne is not blocking the route to the door.]

ANNE: *Thank you for attending our one-to-one to review your progress, I'm interested to find out how things are. So, how are you?*

CHLOE: *I'm not bad... I'm trying my best to get all of the work done but I've had so much to do lately... that I've been struggling a bit to get all of my homework and coursework in on time, but I got most of it in.*

ANNE: *It sounds like it's been hard going for you. But as you say, you did get most of it in, so well done!*

CHLOE: *Thanks, it has been a bit of a struggle for me lately.*

ANNE: *What are the reasons for it being a struggle?*

CHLOE: *Well to be honest, I've been having some problems at home which have been affecting my studies.*

ANNE: *Okay, do you want to tell me about them?*

CHLOE: *Erm, well... okay. I've been having lots of arguments with my stepmum... and it's been really upsetting my dad. We've been falling out a lot and I've not been able to concentrate on my studies all of the time when I've needed to.*

[Anne and Chloe continue to discuss these issues. They both agree some small actions that Chloe can take to help her situation and her studies. They agree to review these in the next one-to-one meeting.]

ANNE: *Okay, let's review your previous agreed targets. For history, you had a target of handing in two exam questions for marking as well as achieving over 60 per cent in the end of unit test. Did you get the exam questions in?*

CHLOE: *Yes, I've had them marked and have discussed the feedback with my teacher. I did okay in them but I now know what I need to do better next time.*

ANNE: *That's good, well done. Make sure you note all of this feedback down so you can refer back to it when you begin revision. I can see that you achieved 58 per cent in the test, how do you feel about that?*

CHLOE: *I'm a bit disappointed to be honest. I did revise, but not as much as I probably could have. We have another test coming up in four weeks which I want to do better in.*

ANNE: *Okay, on a scale of one to ten, where ten is maximum effort, how much effort did you put into the revision?*

CHLOE: *Erm... six.*

ANNE: *So, what can you do to bring that up to a seven?*

CHLOE: *I think I could comfortably do an hour for two evenings a week as I did before.*

ANNE: *Okay. How about we set you a more stretching target of doing an hour for three evenings a week? You've done really well so far to get the 58 per cent but I think you've got the potential to do even better next time.*

CHLOE: *Er... okay. I'll give it a go, I guess.*

[Anne and Chloe continue to agree SMART targets for the rest of her subjects. Anne asks Chloe to summarise her targets after they have been agreed.]

ANNE: *Looking forward, we've agreed your targets and I'd like to see how you are getting on with these when we have our next one-to-one meeting on the 4th of March. Does this sound fair to you?*

CHLOE: *Yes, that's fine.*

ANNE: *Well, thank you for this chat. I know you're facing a few obstacles but you've done really well so far and I believe in you. If you continue to push yourself, you can do even better.*

CHLOE: *Thanks, I hope so.*

Critical thinking activity 8

» *Examine whether your three points from Critical thinking activity 7 have been addressed.*

Dos and don'ts for one-to-ones

Table 4.6 *Suggested dos and don'ts for one to ones*

Dos	Don'ts
Prepare for them, for example by reading previous one-to-ones, at-risk meeting documents, 'staff comments about learners' and speaking to other personal tutors, teachers and support staff about progress.	Be unprepared, because poor preparation or none at all may lead to issues being missed, therefore reducing the impact of the meeting.
Appear pleased to see the learners and have a sincere and calm approach.	Let it appear to the learners that you are just 'ticking off' your one-to-ones as a administrative duty you must fulfil.
Explain at the start of the meeting what things you would like to cover, but ensure you are clear that learners can discuss anything they would like to as well.	Go straight into reviewing the targets without some opportunity for discussion about how the learners are feeling both within and outside the institution.
Use more open questions to allow learners and yourself to explore their thoughts and feelings.	Use more closed questions, because this will elicit only brief answers which don't help to build rapport or understand and explore issues deeply.

Table 4.6 (cont.)

Dos	Don'ts
Record the conversation using the institution's electronic (or alternative) system for future reference.	Focus more on the recording of the conversation than on the quality and depth of the discussion.
Sit near and facing the learner. Facing them slightly at an angle is preferable.	• Have tables between you. • Sit in a way that blocks access to the door. • Shut the door of the room (this could leave you vulnerable to false allegations of inappropriate behaviour). • Be too close so as to invade their personal space.
Display active listening, as well as body language and tone of voice that show you are genuinely interested. Also, use challenging, reframing and reflecting back, and summarising where appropriate.	Appear unengaged in the conversation.
Start with and praise the positive things that the learners have, or feel they have, tried or achieved.	Ignore their positives or be too general.
Be honest about any areas that the learners need to improve.	Start with or ignore areas for development.
Be clear about the consequences of not improving.	Fail to explain the consequences of not improving.
Encourage the learners to reflect and have a clear, open and honest discussion about progress against previous SMART targets (these may be academic, attendance, punctuality, behavioural or personal).	Briefly mention previous SMART targets and offer no opportunity for discussion around these.
Allow the discussion to develop SMART targets that are stretching but are agreed between you and the learners.	Set targets for the learners which you have not discussed or agreed, because this will reduce the level of ownership that they feel for them.
Use scaling and solution-focused coaching techniques where appropriate (more of which in Chapter 6).	
Make clear your desire to help resolve any problems where it is possible.	
Ensure that the agreed targets are SMART.	
Finish on a positive and ask the learner to summarise the agreed targets before the end of the meeting.	
Ensure dates for the review of these targets are agreed before the meeting finishes.	

Critical thinking activity 9

» *Concentrating on the dos from Table 4.6, tick those that you use regularly and describe how you will employ the others from now on.*

A final thought on one-to-ones

As with teaching and lesson planning, there isn't a secret formula for a perfect one-to-one. Within your busy personal tutor role, to avoid spending too much time on detailed planning or recording, it is useful to use the dos and don'ts as a helpful checklist (particularly the dos). As every learner and educational institution is different, your one-to-ones will be different too. You will need to be adaptable to the needs and context of every learner as well as the resources available, and to keep in mind the boundaries discussed in Chapter 3. Carrying out outstanding one-to-ones with learners is a skill that can be learned through practice and reflection, and as you get better the impact on your learners' progress and outcomes will improve.

Group tutorial planning and teaching

Group tutorial planning and teaching is the third and final activity that we explore in this chapter.

Since, usually, there is no qualification linked to the outcome of group tutorials, the whole thing can feel a bit less prescribed than your curriculum lesson delivery. Some institutions deliver smaller and shorter qualifications through group tutorial sessions which are normally built into the learner's study programme, although this isn't the norm.

So, what is the purpose of group tutorials? There is no perfect answer to this question because the purpose and model for delivery can differ between institutions. However, there are two general key purposes that are consistent:

1. The management of the learner; proactively and reactively addressing any issues with ABC, with the aim of reducing barriers to learning, which will positively impact on institutional KPIs.

2. The development and support of the learner; for example, developing employability skills (employment searches, UCAS, presentation and interview skills, CV writing, skill portfolio building), as well as focusing on more pastoral areas such as emotional well-being.

No single delivery model is the correct one. It should be flexible to meet the needs of your learner cohort. However, it is important to make the purpose of the group tutorial sessions clear to the learners when they start and to explain the relevance to their course, career pathway (if they know it) and wider lives. Group tutorials provide another opportunity for you to co-ordinate the learner journey, with the aim of enhancing the learner experience and helping to improve learner outcomes, such as success rates, value-added, internal progression and the destination they progress to when they eventually leave the institution.

Critical thinking activity 10

» *The following short checklist of points (adapted from an article by David Didau, entitled 'Planning a "Perfect" Lesson' (Didau, 2012, online)) can contribute to delivering effective and engaging teaching, learning and assessment. Using this checklist, identify the similarities and differences between what you believe is good curriculum lesson delivery and good group tutorial delivery.*

Table 4.7 *Good curriculum lesson delivery*

PLANNING
The lesson plan relates to the sequence of teaching.
The lesson plan has high expectation and challenge for all learners.
The lesson plan is appropriate for the needs of all learners and includes a situational analysis, which includes information about your group, such as overview of the progress so far and any additional support needs or special considerations.
START
The lesson gets off to a bright start. There is likely to be a recap of previous learning.
Learning objectives are clear, appropriate and shared with the learners.
DURING
The teaching engages the learners and holds their interest.
The teaching meets a range of abilities.
There are a variety of learning activities and opportunities for paired or collaborative work.
Effective use of different types of questioning and clear feedback on progress is given.
All learners are actively involved.
Learner knowledge and understanding are increased, as well as the opportunity for learners to demonstrate this.
Opportunities to develop learners' English, mathematics and functional skills are taken.
END
The learning objectives are reviewed and questions are used to check learning has taken place.
Evidence of learner self-assessment of progress.
Feedback is given to the learners on their progress. There may also be learner-to-learner feedback.
The next lesson or lessons are previewed, in other words learners are able to 'look forward'.

Discussion

You can hopefully see that there are many more common elements between good curriculum lesson and group tutorial delivery than there are differences. It is important that you don't feel the need to tick off the entire checklist in order to deliver a good group tutorial (or lesson). However, it is a useful guide for good delivery. Essentially, the principles of good teaching are pretty much the same whether you are delivering a curriculum lesson or a group tutorial.

The key differences are as follows.

- Group tutorials tend to be shorter, therefore this should be taken into account in your planning, particularly the learning objectives, activities and assessment methods.

- There isn't normally a qualification attached to group tutorials; therefore, this will reduce the frequency of certain assessment methods, for example tests, mock exams, marking of assignments or exam questions.

- There is more opportunity to be flexible to the immediate needs of the group, for example relating the content to issues such as bullying incidents, bereavement, drugs, pregnancy, and economic or political issues.

- There can be greater flexibility, meaning you may want to consider some different learning activities or room layout, for example:

  o have the room with the chairs in a circle and no tables. This will allow for open discussion, similar to therapy rather than content delivery. Experience has shown that when used frequently, this works particularly well with lower-level learners to draw out any issues they are facing, for example asking them to say one good thing and one bad thing that has happened this week. Be sensitive to those learners who don't want to contribute. If they normally contribute but don't want to, this could be an indicator of an issue that you may want to approach later in a one-to-one discussion;

  o if learners are being given back, or have brought, marked work (for example assignments or exam questions), it is useful to provide an opportunity for them to reflect on the work they have done or the feedback from their teacher (although this may have been done already in the lesson). Ways to do this include:

  o individual reflection – allow learners time to reread their work and ask them to write down three things they did well and three things they need to do better next time;

  o peer reflection – pair learners up and ask them to read each other's work and then discuss with their partner three things they did well and three things they could do better next time. This needs to be managed carefully in terms of the sensitivity of learners analysing each other's work and usually works best when it isn't done with their friends and is mixed up by ability.

Content to be covered in group tutorials

The content that you cover is usually flexible (depending on your institution) to meet the needs of your learners. Since all institutions are different and the learners within them are divided by vocational or general education (A levels) and, if vocational, are further divided by subject area and level, the following suggested group tutorial content covers themes that can be adapted and differentiated as appropriate. You may already have group tutorial content set; however, the following acts as a useful guide.

We start with introductory topics but the rest could be reordered chronologically. As such, it's not exactly the same as a scheme of work but, rather, you can use it like a curriculum course specification from which you can develop your own group tutorial scheme of work. It's also necessary to recognise the natural overlap between the sections and the importance of revisiting topics or themes, just as you would do within the curriculum; for example, reflection (theme 3) has a strong link to actions and consequences (within theme 7).

The National Occupational Standards (NOS) for Personal Tutoring set out good practice in personal tutoring and thus are relevant to group tutorial content. The 11 standards cover:

1. *Manage self, work relationships and work demands.*

2. *Develop own practice in personal tutoring.*

3. *Create a safe, supportive and positive learning environment.*

4. *Explore and identify learners' needs and address barriers to learning.*

5. *Enable learners to set learning targets and evaluate their progress and achievement.*

6. *Encourage the development of learner autonomy.*

7. *Enable learners to develop personal and social skills and cultural awareness.*

8. *Enable learners to enhance learning and employability skills.*

9. *Support learners' transition and progression.*

10. *Provide learner access to specialist support services.*

11. *Contribute to improving the quality and impact of personal tutoring and its reputation within own organisation.*

(UK Commission for Education and Skills, n.d., online)

Table 4.8 Group tutorial content

	Themes and topics	Suggested learner outcomes	Possible learner activity	Link to NOS
1	Introduction to your institution, expectations and procedures Introduction to: • The institution; • tutorial and support; • policies and procedures; • anti-bullying; • learner voice; • complaints procedure; • electronic tracking and monitoring systems.	Familiarise yourself with: • The institution; • tutorial and support; • policies and procedures. Identify the key points of relevant policies and describe their relevance to you. Identify your learner representatives. Identify the support mechanisms available to you.	*Small group work on policies – each group to produce a poster on a different procedure with key points.*	NOS 3 NOS 5 NOS 10
2	Developing yourself – being independent and responsible • Being independent; • taking responsibility; • SMART targets; • being resilient.	• Set effective goals for yourself; • create your own SMART targets; • identify ways you can cope with failure and how this eventually can help you succeed.		NOS 6
3	Developing yourself – being reflective Reflection skills: • Thinking about your experiences and actions inside and outside the institution; • using this to plan future actions.	• Define reflection and understand its purpose; • distinguish between effective and ineffective reflection; • produce examples of reflective practice.		NOS 6

4	**Your skills** Study skills. Skills self-assessment – identifying your strengths and areas for development. Including: • Teamwork; • employability skills; • communication skills; • planning and organisational skills.	• List and define key study skills; • identify existing or potential barriers to your learning; • self-assess: identify your own skills, strengths and areas for development; • practise your communication skills for different situations – presenting to others, contributing to discussion, effective listening, non-verbal communication.	NOS 4 NOS 5 NOS 6
5	**Your next step** • Progression; • career plan; • higher education; • UCAS.	• Identify your progression routes; • produce a career timeline and plan; • produce an effective personal statement (employment route and university route); • understand the UCAS application system and process; • produce a UCAS application.	NOS 9
6	**Your health and well-being** • Alcohol use; • drug use; • sexual health; • mental health; • self-esteem and self-image; • hygiene.	Identify and describe the key points related to your health and well-being.	NOS 7

Table 4.8 (cont.)

	Themes and topics	Suggested learner outcomes	Possible learner activity	Link to NOS
7	Respect • Rights and responsibilities; • actions and consequences; • conflict resolution; • your personal safety; • what safeguarding means; • anti-bullying (revisit); • staying safe online.	Understand and describe your rights and responsibilities. Link specific consequences to specific actions. Apply conflict resolution strategies. Describe the key points about keeping yourself safe.		NOS 3
8	Managing your money Finance and budgeting.	• Be able to use calculations to make spending choices; • understand the link between personal financial budgets and spending choices; • know the consequences associated with spending and borrowing.		NOS 7
9	Being a positive member of society • How you contribute positively to society; • your social and cultural awareness; • british values (for a definition of these values, see the *Prevent Strategy* listed in Taking it further).	• Identify and describe how you can be a positive member of society; • identify relevant social and cultural issues; • understand and articulate British values; • contribute to discussion of social and cultural issues.		NOS 7

Each has its own 'knowledge and understanding' and 'performance criteria' descriptors which are too lengthy to state here, but they can be found in their entirety at http://nos. ukces.org.uk.

We revisit the standards in Chapter 9 (on measuring impact). The final column of Table 4.8 states the relevant standard for each theme.

Critical thinking activity 11

1. Using Table 4.8 identify any topics you think need adding and any you think are less important for your learners.

2. Complete the fourth column stating possible learner activities for each theme (an example is included in italics).

3. Using these learner activities, with a particular class in mind, plan a group tutorial session on any topic from Table 4.8, which is fully contextualised within the (or a) subject area the group is studying.

Group tutorial contextualisation

Experience shows that group tutorial delivery (as well as the tracking and monitoring of learners and one-to-ones) works best when it is embedded within the overall institution's strategy for learning, along with being tailored to the subject area the learners are studying. Tailoring the content to be specific to particular industries or career pathways helps to improve the relevance and enjoyment for the learner as well as the impact on their career prospects. A simple example could be that, if you are covering content related to the wider economy in a brickwork or built environment group tutorial, bring in statistics related to the construction industry and the effect on the recruitment of construction workers.

Differentiation

You will no doubt be familiar with the concept of differentiation and be employing some differentiation techniques already. These may include modification of:

*   the dialogue and support you give to each learner;

*   the tasks you set them;

*   the pace learners can work at individually;

*   the way you group the learners;

*   the resources you use;

*   the outcomes you expect or find acceptable.

Differentiating for group tutorial isn't really any different, although, since there isn't usually a qualification being assessed, differentiating through assessment is likely to be used less frequently.

It is important to differentiate the content within group tutorials for two main reasons. To ensure:

1.   it is accessible and relevant for the level of learner you are working with;

2.   that, as learners progress through levels, the content and activities offer appropriate variety and depth, especially when there is a chance they may cover the same or a similar topic again.

Summary

In this chapter we have looked in detail at some of the key activities of the personal tutor role which are integral to your practice and should be central within the strategy for learning in your institution.

We have looked at the tracking and monitoring of learners. Many factors will influence the effectiveness of your tracking and monitoring. One of them is the relationship you have with your colleagues. When you are developing actions for learners who are underperforming, not all staff will have the same view. Some may think that a firmer approach is needed, while others may think a softer approach will work best. Agreeing a way forward isn't always a 'straight line' and this subjectivity is something you must learn to manage through your influencing skills. Remember, however, that everyone has the right to a view but not everyone's view will be right. It is your responsibility to allow these individual perceptions to inform your holistic interpretation of each learner's performance and support needs, while ensuring that the actions that you and others take always have learners' success and well-being at the centre of them.

Learning checklist

Tick off each point when you feel confident you understand it.

☐   *I recognise that regularly tracking and monitoring the progress of each of my learners is one of the key activities in the pursuit of improving their success.*

☐   *I realise some of my learners may have background characteristics (either from their past or which develop during their time in the institution) which may raise the chances of them being at risk or vulnerable.*

☐   *I know that, as the academic year progresses and each learner's situation changes, the at risk category and the support provided should change accordingly.*

☐   *I recognise that tracking and monitoring of learners should not be solely focused on learners who may be at risk of failing or withdrawing from their course; it should be equally focused on learners who may be at risk of not achieving their target grades.*

☐   *I recognise that regularly speaking to my colleagues and using the institution's electronic learner tracking and monitoring system is important to inform my holistic view of each learner's progress.*

☐ *I recognise the elements of an effective one-to-one: that I should be well prepared and that it should be a two-way conversation where the learner does the majority of the thinking and talking (in other words is active, not passive).*

☐ *I can identify the two main purposes for group tutorial which are, firstly, the management of the learner and, secondly, the development and support of the learner, as well as focusing on more pastoral areas, such as emotional well-being.*

☐ *I appreciate that there are more common elements between good curriculum lesson and group tutorial delivery than there are differences and that the principles of good teaching are very similar whether you are delivering a lesson or a group tutorial.*

Critical reflections

1. Analyse the importance that your institution places on tracking and monitoring learner progress (if you have taught at more than one institution, compare and contrast the two institutions' approaches, using examples). What are the positive points about the methods they use and what things could they improve?

2. Evaluate:

   a. how you feel electronic systems may have improved the tracking and monitoring of learner progress compared to traditional paper-based systems;

   b. how this may have changed the impact of the personal tutor role.

3. Using Figure 4.3 as a guide (whether you have an electronic system or not):

   a. identify your strengths and points for development in the tracking and monitoring of your learners;

   b. set yourself two development targets to work on over the next six weeks. On completion, critically review your progress.

4. What is your view on the relative importance of one-to-one meetings compared to group tutorials in enabling learners to succeed? Do you think your colleagues, and more widely your institution, have a similar view?

5. From your experience of group tutorials, explain how much of your time is spent on managing the learner and how much is spent on developing and supporting the learner, including pastoral activities. Which factors influenced how you divided your time?

Personal tutor self-assessment system

The key activities for the personal tutor are:

- the tracking and monitoring of learners;
- one-to-ones with learners;
- group tutorial planning and teaching.

PERSONAL TUTOR SELF-ASSESSMENT SYSTEM: Chapter 4 the learner experience: key activities

	Minimum standard 2 points	Bronze 4 points	Silver 6 points	Gold 8 points	Platinum 10 points
Individual	I ensure that all of the key activities are fully thought through and planned before they begin.	I regularly reflect to identify strengths and areas for development related to the key activities. I build these into my future planning and discuss them with my line manager during appraisal meetings.	I regularly ask for learner feedback on how effective my employment of the key activities is. I hold formal end-of-year reviews with relevant colleagues to identify strengths and areas for development. I arrange for peer-observation opportunities for my one-to-ones and group tutorials.	Feedback from my learners regarding the key activities is consistently very positive. Feedback from colleagues shows they regard them as having a strong impact on learner progress and outcomes.	I identify and implement methods to measure the impact of the key activities on my learners' progress and outcomes.
Institutional	My institution has the key activities embedded into its strategy for learning.	The strategy for learning is effectively communicated to all new staff and updates for existing staff are frequent. One-to-ones and group tutorials are observed alongside lessons through my institution's observation scheme.	The key activities are routinely discussed in all delivery staff's appraisal meetings.	Feedback from the majority of learners shows that the key activities fully support their needs. There are frequent opportunities organised for staff to share good practice related to the key activities.	Relevant data on key performance indicators is used to systematically review the strengths and areas for development of the key activities. This analysis feeds into a rigorous departmental self-assessment system and the outcome is SMART quality improvement plans.

The self-assessment system is available as a free download from the publisher's website and the authors' websites (all listed at the start of the book).

Taking it further

The Education and Economic Development Coordinating Council At-Risk Student Committee (n.d.) *At-Risk Student Intervention Implementation Guide*. Particularly pp 13–15.

Prevent Strategy (2011). Available at: www.gov.uk/government/publications/prevent-strategy-2011 [accessed July 2015]. This contains further information about British values.

Bullock, K and Fertig, M (2005) Partners in learning or monitors for attendance? Views on personal tutorials from FE in *Research in Post-Compulsory Education* 8 (2): 279–93.

Wisker, G, Exley, K, Antoniou, M and Ridley, P (2007) *Working One-to-One with Students: Supervising, Coaching, Mentoring, and Personal Tutoring (Key Guides for Effective Teaching in Higher Education)*. Oxon: Routledge.

References

Crace, J (2002) *Personal Touch: Tutorials Get Good Results – If the Tutor Does Their Homework*. [online] Available at: www.theguardian.com/education/2002/feb/05/furthereducation.uk5 [accessed May 2015].

Didau, D (2012) *Planning a 'Perfect'Lesson*. [online] Available at: www.learningspy.co.uk/education/planning-a-perfect-lesson/ [accessed May 2015].

The Education and Economic Development Coordinating Council At-Risk Student Committee (n.d.) *At-Risk Student Intervention Implementation Guide*.

UK Commission For Education and Skills (n.d.) *National Occupational Standards for Personal Tutoring*. [online] Available: http://nos.ukces.org.uk/Pages/index.aspx [accessed May 2015].

The National Commission on Excellence in Education (1983) *A Nation At Risk: The Imperative For Educational Reform. A Report to the Nation and the Secretary of Education, United States Department of Education*.

5 The learner experience: key procedures

Chapter aims

This chapter helps you to:

- understand how policies and procedures relate to each other;
- identify the institutional procedures most relevant to the personal tutor role
  - disciplinary – a positive approach
  - right course review
  - internal progression
  - external progression
  - working with learners who have additional support needs
  - safeguarding;
- understand the working of these procedures, your role within them and the impact on learners;
- recognise the importance of dividing responsibility within these procedures;
- develop your knowledge and language of key procedures in order to critically reflect and review them.

Introduction

Questions I remember asking a lot when I first started teaching and being a personal tutor were, 'So what's the procedure on...?' or, 'Do we have a policy on...?' Since curriculum procedures in my subject area were something we talked about as a team all the time, these questions in particular came up in relation to the support side. This chapter gives you a clear picture of what these procedures are and, crucially, what your role is within them. We have chosen the procedures we deem to be most relevant to you. Institutions may have different ways of labelling the procedures we look at in this chapter, but there shouldn't be too much difficulty in recognising the ones we are talking about.

What is a *procedure*? The term is quite often confused with *policy*. This is perfectly understandable because the two are closely related. Policies inform the practice that takes place within the institution, but often they are public documents for external audiences which need to cover all eventualities on a topic or theme and thus can be lengthy, wordy and cumbersome. Procedures interpret that policy in a more useable, shorter, step-by-step form. For example, your institution will have a disciplinary policy; but if you have a disciplinary flow chart on the staffroom wall, this is the interpretation of that policy in a procedure for day-to-day use.

Disciplinary: a positive approach

Critical thinking activity 1

Think of a time in your childhood when you misbehaved or did something wrong and the person addressing you about this behaviour did this well. Think of another occasion when you misbehaved or did something wrong and the person addressing you about this behaviour did so poorly.

1. Make two lists; one showing the ways the person in the former situation acted and a second which does the same for the person in the latter scenario.

2. For each point try to state what effect this had on you personally, and in particular what effect it had on your future behaviour.

Discussion

Of course, what constitutes 'done well' and 'done poorly' is subjective and could be an oversimplistic division. For example, even if you didn't agree with the approach but it made you never repeat the misbehaviour, does that make the approach good or bad? This depends on whether or not repeating the action is the only measure of the success of the approach. Also, would another wrongdoer have responded in the same way? So, a further meaningful question may be: which positive, non-punitive approaches are most likely to prevent repetition of the behaviour for the majority of people? To understand this we consider research and our experience. Leaving those discussions to one side for the moment, you may have come up with some answers similar to those shown in Table 5.1. We have called the person addressing the wrongdoing the admonisher.

Table 5.1 *Admonishers' approaches to poor behaviour*

Situation 1	
Approach of the admonisher	**Effect**
Discussed, with me, why I did it.	• Increased understanding of the action. • Increased ability to articulate feelings.
Showed me the effect it had on others.	• Promoted empathy. • Increased understanding of the consequences of the action.
Ensured I acted afterwards, for example apologised to those affected.	• Taking responsibility. • Built positive relationships.
Forgiveness, alongside ensuring the lessons were understood.	• Improved self-assurance and feelings of security. • Increased ability to learn from mistakes.
Situation two	
Approach of the admonisher	**Effect**
Aggressive response with no discussion.	• Fear of authority. • Limited or no learning from the situation.
Punishment without forgiveness.	• Fear of authority. • Reduced confidence and increased insecurity.
No real response; let me 'get away with it'.	• No learning from the situation. • No appreciation of consequences.

In the main, the key differences in the experience of the wrong-doer between the two situations can be summarised as *rehabilitation* in situation 1 as opposed to *retribution* in situation 2. It is situation 1 that a positive approach to disciplinary is concerned with. In other words, it is to positively engage a learner in order to effect behavioural change without using punitive measures.

What do we mean by 'poor behaviour'?

It is also important to briefly consider what we mean by the different terms relating to learner behaviour. Wallace (2013a) helpfully draws out the subtle differences between the following three terms.

- 'Disengagement' – where learners have detached themselves from the idea of formal learning.

- 'Non-compliance' – examples include frequent absence from lessons, lack of punctuality, failure to complete or hand in work, refusal to contribute usefully to discussions or activities and failure to listen to what the teacher or others are saying.

- 'Challenging behaviour' – for example, a point blank refusal to obey an instruction from a teacher to do something like to sit down, put their phone away or turn their chair to face the front.

(adapted from Wallace, 2013a, p 88)

She makes the important point that these three are not synonymous but, rather, *'represent a sequence of escalating cause and effect'* (Wallace, 2013a, p 88). Thinking about which behaviour you are faced with will help you to take the most appropriate approach.

Does research say a positive approach works?

Cotton (2010) researched alternatives to detentions in schools to address incidents of poor behaviour. Two schools with children experiencing social emotional behavioural difficulties (SEBD) used the '3 Ls' approach as an alternative to detentions:

- listen to the learner's point of view;

- link the feelings to the behaviour;

- learn better reactions for the next time you have that feeling.

(adapted from Cotton, 2010, p 28)

Both schools saw a reduction in incidents over a 12-week period, and one school experienced a reduction of 51 per cent (Cotton, 2013a, p 17). In a further study, Cotton designed an app for learners to use, based on the 3 Ls approach, *'to help learners recognise that feelings drive behaviour and more appropriate behaviours can be exhibited to show how the learner is feeling'* (Cotton, 2013a, p 24). A 64.5 per cent reduction in behaviour incidents was seen during the research (Cotton, 2013a, p 43). The research showed that rather than staff and institutions seeking to control behaviour, it is much more effective to enable learners to learn to control their own behaviour using positive listening and learning techniques.

Interestingly, Wallace (2013a, p 355) found that a positive teacher–learner relationship and the attitude and demeanour of the teacher had more success in encouraging positive behaviour than any other prescribed strategies. Specific observed situations included the following descriptions: *'chatted with him in a freindly [sic] way'*; *'didn't get mad but showed he was concerned in a nice way'*; *'firm but made it obvious she was being kind and caring'* (Wallace, 2013a, p 355).

Learners may describe you in the same way if you use the tools discussed here because they have positive relationship building at their core and, indeed, are structured in such a way for this to happen.

Tools to get your learners back on track

What are the specific tools to help you to re-engage your learners? We've looked at the general positive approaches to addressing poor behaviour and seen some particular actions carried out in research. Although in a slightly different form, there is much common ground between these and the tools we will now outline.

Table 5.2 Tools to get your learners back on track

Tool	Aim	Explanation	When to use
Positive learning conversation (PLC)	To uncover underlying reasons for poor attendance (including punctuality), behaviour or completion of work (ABC) and thus re-engage the learner and effect a behavioural change.	An individual meeting between the personal tutor and learner to discuss issues with attendance, behaviour or completion of work (ABC). It could be one, a combination or all three of these. Use the key principles of an effective one-to-one with a learner from Chapter 4 but with the added dimension of purposefully trying to effect a positive behavioural change, and the SMART targets set should reflect this. You may wish to request a manager to be present if appropriate.	With a learner whose standards of attendance, behaviour or completion of work (ABC) has fallen below the institution's expected standards. A useful guideline is to use after two or three 'causes for concern' from teachers. Use before formal disciplinary stages at manager level.
Positive learning conversation review	To review whether the targets set in the PLC have been achieved.	If PLC review targets are repeatedly not met, the learner can be referred to the formal disciplinary process at manager level. Again, you may wish to request a manager to be present if appropriate.	Shortly after the PLC, depending on the issue. A useful guideline is one to two weeks after the PLC.
Learner report	To effect a behavioural change in a learner who needs lesson-by-lesson monitoring.	A report, co-ordinated by you, where a learner's teachers feedback to you about the learner's ABC over a period of one or two weeks.	In isolation or can work well alongside a PLC or when a formal disciplinary meeting has taken place and where showing improvements from the report have been set as a condition of continuing on the course.
Mediation ('restorative justice')	Restore justice/repair relationships/heal hurt feelings between learners or between learners and staff.	A meeting of learners between whom there has been disagreement/gossiping/bullying. You as personal tutor and possibly other staff are present. Rules of the meeting include: • only one person to talk at a time; • each person to be able to state their points; • all views respected; • no raising of voices; • keeping as calm as possible.	After a bullying incident or conflict situation between fellow learners or learner(s) and a member of staff.

The case for a positive approach to disciplinary

The rationale for all of these tools is to dig down to the underlying reasons for poor standards of ABC and to provide positive reinforcement to learners (some of whom may have never experienced this before). As Wallace (2013a, p 95) states, '*What looks like simply a lack of respect may be a signal that something more complex needs addressing in terms of the learner's needs*'. Reading and interpreting learner behaviour and seeing it as a way of communicating in order to understand what it is telling us (Wallace, 2013a) is key.

It is important to emphasise that this goes hand in hand with the aim of encouraging the learner to take ownership and responsibility. As we've seen through the research discussed, positive strategies, which include conversations with the learner to address these issues, affect behavioural change and can reduce the number of incidents far more than simple, punitive measures. You should still be robust when addressing ABC issues and have tight rules and clear procedures.

So, the aim of these tools and strategies is not for us to control learner behaviour but for learners to eventually take ownership and control it themselves. As Cotton states, '*negative consequences drive negative feelings which in turn drive negative behaviours*' (Cotton, 2013a, p 3). A positive approach to learners with ABC issues, and employment of its strategies, seeks to change each of these negatives into positives.

Critical thinking activity 2

» *Look at the case study testimony from Joe, a learner who had significant attendance and behaviour issues in the first term but showed great improvements in the second. Which tool has been used by Selina, his personal tutor, and what specific techniques are evident?*

CASE STUDY

Joe's testimony

I was always off college last term and when I was there I mucked about a lot. At school we just got detention for stuff like that where we had to sit with other bad students and do nothing. It's well different at college though. My tutor Selina, she sat me down and talked to me about it. She didn't tell me off or, like, tell me much about what she thought about it or anything, she just asked questions like what's happening... why's that... tell me more... and things like that. She got out of me the real reason I'd been missing college... working loads at Matalan to get the money for going out nearly every night which I'd just got into in a big way. That was what was most important to me at the time but speaking to Selina about what I wanted to do long-term... my ideal future... a business apprenticeship... made me realise how much more important that was and the way I was going at college might stop me getting it. It wasn't just a chat either... she typed up really specific things I had to do... even like not going out on Tuesday and Wednesday nights... and sent a copy of this home to my mum who kept reminding me! I knew she'd check I'd done them in a couple of weeks too. I remember she also showed me a reference for an apprenticeship employer for a good student compared to one for a bad student. I'd had the odd thing like that at school before on top of detention but this time I wanted to change whereas before I didn't see much point.

Discussion

You are likely to have recognised the employment of the positive learning conversation and the techniques of:

* not judging;

* using open questions;

* setting SMART targets;

* organising a review meeting and stating its purpose;

* getting parents/guardians involved;

* enabling the learner to take ownership;

* influencing feelings and beliefs so that learners control their own behaviour
(Cotton, 2013a).

The last point is the overall aim of the techniques that precede it.

The formal disciplinary process

As we've seen, positive learning conversations and reviews precede formal disciplinary stages. In Chapter 3 where we discussed boundaries, we talked about your need to refer upwards once your support has been exhausted, and essentially it's the same message here: formal procedures need to be used when you, through your positive approach, have taken learners as far as they can go. It is not always absolutely clear when that point is reached, but it is something to be determined by discussion with your line manager or trusted colleagues.

We suggest the personal tutor shouldn't have absolute responsibility for carrying out the formal disciplinary process; however, you might be required to be involved with it. In most institutions, meetings and hearings take place at various levels (according to severity) and, since you are often the person who knows that learner best, you may well be required to attend. If this is the case, it is important that your institution, or the manager who is chairing the meeting, clarifies your role within these. To avoid confusion for the learner and yourself over who the disciplinarian is, it is good practice for you to act as advocate for the learner. In other words you ensure the learner is represented accurately (since they may not have these skills) and that a 'fair hearing' takes place while, at the same time, remaining neutral over any disciplinary action that may be taken.

Right course review

Background

At an early age, young people in Britain have to make fairly big choices affecting their future. In comparison to some other countries there is a greater specificity of subject, both in general and vocational education. In terms of vocational education, after National Vocational Qualifications (NVQs) were introduced in 1986, a wider curriculum (involving some 'general' studies such as the discussion of social issues) was stopped for vocational learners (Wallace, 2013a). Some researchers have argued for a model closer to the German dual system (Wallace, 2013a), also used in other countries, where apprenticeships in a company are combined with vocational education in a vocational school, and the curriculum is broader rather than exclusively skills based.

There are also the issues of guidance and lack of alternative. As Fuller and Macfayden (2012, p 351) state, '*lack of adequate guidance or a failure to be chosen to stay on at school – may result in learners finding themselves, by default, in FE colleges on vocational programmes they have not in any real sense "chosen"*'.

Moreover, research studies into the reasons for learners withdrawing (in other words 'dropping out') from further education institutions show that they tend to be less satisfied with the suitability of their course than learners who complete (Martinez, 2001, p 3). It's important to note that this is only one among a number of reasons given which cover the broad aspects of a learner's experience in college, including '*the intrinsic interest of their course, timetabling issues, the overall quality of teaching, help and support received from teachers*' (Martinez, 2001, p 3). Nevertheless, its appearance on the list, along with the bigger picture just outlined, shows how important right course review is.

What is right course review?

As the title suggests, right course review is a process to check that learners are on the right course in terms of their enjoyment and long-term aims. Right course review is also about giving the young person the tools to make those big decisions. The term is just one of those used in the sector to describe this process. Your own institution may phrase it differently.

Why should you do right course review?

Table 5.3 Reasons for right course review

Perspective	Reasons for learners being on the right course
Learner	• Ethically, learners need to be on the right course – the institution makes a commitment to this guidance and support. • Increased motivation – linked to good behaviour and positive group dynamics.
Personal tutor	• More efficient use of temporal (time) boundary.

Table 5.3 (cont.)

Perspective	Reasons for learners being on the right course
Department	• Will have a positive effect on departmental performance indicators – retention, success, attendance and punctuality, value-added and internal progression.
Institution	• Will have a positive effect on overall performance indicators – retention, success, attendance and punctuality, value-added and internal progression – some of which are linked to government funding.

When do you do right course review?

Those working in colleges will have heard of 'day 42'. If a learner leaves a course after this date, the institution can lose its funding for that learner and there is a negative effect on success rates. Any learners wanting and needing to transfer courses need to do this at an early stage within term one so that they do not miss too much learning. From all perspectives, then, it is clear that it has to happen prior to this. Indeed, we can say that the process even begins before learners start their course. It is good practice in institutions to carry out 'transition' at the end of the academic year to prepare new, and sometimes progressing, learners for their course the following September (see Figure 4.1 in Chapter 4). Learners will have a taster of their course and its expectations, and an important part of this time is for them to check they are on the right course and feel confident to speak up if they think they are not.

Since transition provides so many benefits for the learner, yourself as the personal tutor, other staff and the institution, if this is not part of your institution's calendar currently, it would be a good idea to lobby your manager for it to be included.

As a process in its own right though, right course review takes place early in term one, for example in week four of teaching. In fact, it is a good idea to carry this out *throughout* term one, with many staff informally but persistently checking that learners are on the right course. As such, right course review can be a collaborative process, although most institutions will expect you, as tutor, to carry out the review.

How do you carry out right course review?

Critical thinking activity 3

» *Look at the case study dialogue from a one-to-one meeting between Paul, who is on level 2 science, and his personal tutor Liz, which is taking place in week four. Identify helpful behaviours that enable Paul to form a decision about the right course for him.*

CASE STUDY

Liz's right course review one-to-one with Paul

LIZ: *How's the course going?*

PAUL: *Alright...*

LIZ: *Tell me two things you most enjoy about it.*

PAUL: *Erm... dunno really... looking forward to the trip.*

LIZ: *But anything you've done so far that you've enjoyed...?*

PAUL: *(shrugs)*

LIZ: *How about two things you find hard or have not enjoyed then?*

PAUL: *There's so much writing... and lots of units and topics to cover...*

LIZ: *Okay... it does take hard work to get a qualification sometimes and you have to do those things... what are some of the topics?*

PAUL: *All about cells... chemicals and stuff like that too...*

LIZ: *How do you feel about those topics?*

PAUL: *Not much...*

LIZ: *Okay, let's go back a step... what do you do at home when you're not at college?*

PAUL: *Not a lot... work at Sportsworld, watch TV, look after my little brother and kick boxing club once a week.*

LIZ: *I noticed your face lit up when you mentioned the club... what's so good about that?*

PAUL: *It's just... I right enjoy the challenge, the competition and I'm not bad at it. The bloke who runs it gets me to teach the kids there some of the techniques...*

LIZ: *And you like that teaching part as well as the competition and the keeping fit?*

PAUL: *Yeah, all of it really.*

LIZ: *Interesting. So if you had to list all the things you do outside college and had to say which you enjoy most what would your top two be?*

PAUL: *Kick boxing and... looking after my brother... well most of the time [smiles].*

LIZ: *I know what you mean [smiles]. Do you do much reading or writing at home...?*

PAUL: *Not really...*

LIZ: *What do your parents do?*

PAUL: *My dad's a lab technician.*

LIZ: *And is that where the idea to do science came from?*

PAUL: *Yes.*

LIZ: *Right, okay. If you had to say how much out of ten you enjoy practical and sporting subjects what would you say?*

PAUL: *Probably nine...*

LIZ: *Wow... right, okay. Now do the same for factual, scientific or theory subjects... what would you say?*

PAUL: *It depends...*

LIZ: *On what...?*

PAUL: *If the topic is something I'm interested in then I don't mind doing some theory...*

LIZ: *Ah, okay... can you give me an example?*

PAUL: *Well, this guy at the club told me all about fitness.*

LIZ: *Right, well that's really interesting... You're right, it's not always a clear divide between theory and practical... often there's a mix. What do you think about sports science for example? And there's opportunity for teaching sports in the future with that.*

PAUL: *Sounds good...*

LIZ: *Thinking about when you first came here to transition in July and the first few weeks of the term and all we've said recently about being on the right course, how much, out of ten again, do you think you need to change course?*

PAUL: *Probably eight.*

LIZ: *Right okay. Well obviously I don't want you to feel in any way forced to change but you do need to make sure you're on the right course.*

PAUL: *What about my mum and dad?*

LIZ: *Well, you tell me, how do you think they'll feel about a change?*

PAUL: *Might be not too happy at first but...*

LIZ: *.... after you or I have explained...*

PAUL: *Yeah... they did really want me to do science but it's because what my dad knows... but I reckon they'll be okay...*

LIZ: *Well, they have to be okay about it too... and I will contact them about this chat... they already have an idea things are not great on the course after I spoke to them... y'know... about when you were skipping lessons for the gym...*

PAUL: *Yeah, I know... [smiles].*

LIZ: *It's also not set in stone. Let's go and make an appointment with Mark, the college careers adviser, because he knows more about all the options than me...*

PAUL: *Okay.*

LIZ: *And then can we meet on Friday at 3pm to see if you've made a decision?*

PAUL: *Yeah... will put a reminder in my phone.*

LIZ: *Okay great. How do you feel about college now we've talked about things?*

PAUL: *A lot better actually.*

Discussion

Some helpful behaviours in right course review conversations that we can take from Liz's approach are:

* use of open questions, for example asking the learner to list the most enjoyable and least enjoyable aspects of the course rather than closed questions such as 'are you enjoying your course?' which is likely to elicit a simple 'yes' or 'no';

* try a different tack when information is not forthcoming, for example appeal to life outside college in order to gain a picture of interests;

* use scaling, in other words where you get the learner to mark a statement out of ten (scaling is discussed further in Chapter 6);

* link thoughts or actions to feelings;

* try to uncover underlying reasons for the learner's choice of course;

* emphasise the positives and reassure, thus creating a supportive environment making honest discussion more likely.

Internal progression

What is internal progression and why is it important?

Internal progression refers to the movement of learners to the next level of their course or to the next level of an alternative course, another procedure within which you can play a very important part. Offering clear pathways to learners and achieving high levels of internal progression is desirable for all of the reasons mentioned in the previous section; it is beneficial from a learner, personal tutor, departmental and institutional perspective.

The research studies into the reasons for learners withdrawing from further education institutions previously mentioned, state that another factor they are less than satisfied with in terms of their college experience is '*help in preparing to move on to a job or a higher qualification*' (Martinez, 2001, p 3). As already stated, this shouldn't be viewed as the sole, or most significant, reason for learners leaving an institution (and thus adversely affecting retention), but it does highlight the importance of internal and external progression procedures and your role within them.

A typical internal progression process explained

Institutions will have different internal progression processes which will be a reflection of their internal progression policies. What follows is an explanation of a typical process. It is important to note that internal progression is more related to vocational subjects rather than A level; however, some of the principles of ensuring learners improve from one year to the next are still pertinent.

Table 5.4 A typical internal progression process explained

Feature	Explanation
Timescale	Generally the internal progression process for each academic year should commence at the beginning of the second term when the process is introduced and explained in group tutorials.
Your role	• is to set targets for improvement for those not recommended to progress; • should be as the advocate for the learner; • is to signpost learners who do not have a place having gone through all the procedures. We look at this in the next section on external progression.
Learners currently not recommended to progress	• Generally, institutions will make judgements about whether or not a learner has met the ABC requirements to be able to progress internally. • Even though learners may not automatically be able to progress due to ABC reasons, it is your role to support them to work towards their SMART targets in order to improve their chances of progression. • Clear expectations, SMART target setting, reviewing of targets (against ABC standards) in a reasonable timeframe and engaging all those who influence a learner is the recipe for a holistic approach which aims to ensure the standards of ABC.

Table 5.4 (*cont.*)

Feature	Explanation
Communication	• You should engage with all those who influence a learner in order to achieve a holistic view. • You should set yourself the goal of all learners (and their parents or guardians) knowing clearly what their destination at the end of the academic year is. Due to learners not being recommended to progress, the changing of minds, the liaising with other departmental staff and managers and other issues, this is not always easy to achieve.
A new curriculum area	While the same principle of targets for improvement applies, learners wanting to move to a new curriculum area may be accommodated slightly differently in the sense of being given a 'fresh start' if they have found during the year that their current course is not what they wanted.
Learners taking responsibility	In the context of internal progression, you need to enable the learners to take responsibility through the agreement of their own targets for improvement.

Progression monitoring

In order to keep track of your learners' progression, a live document which can be updated is necessary. These may take different forms in different educational institutions, but usually they have common content.

Critical thinking activity 4

Look at Table 5.5, which shows three learners who are currently not recommended to progress for a variety of reasons. Plan your actions for these learners in order for them to make improvements and potentially be able to progress. Complete the relevant columns of the monitoring document by answering these two questions.

1. What targets for improvement will you set?

2. What other actions will you take and who will you involve?

Discussion

How did you do? Compare your answers to those suggested in Table 5.6.

Table 5.5 *Extract from a progression monitoring document*

Learner name/ current course/ years at college	Recommended? (Y/N)	Intended destination	Reason for non-recommendation	Notes	Targets for improvement	Actions taken and notes
Lewis Parker. Level 2 catering. 1st year.	No.	Level 3 catering.	Attendance (currently 68 per cent).	Mental health issues have affected attendance.		
Amir Hassan. Level 1 joinery. 2nd year.	No.	Level 2 computing.	Attendance (77 per cent). Completion of work.	Made a bullying statement earlier in the year.		
Chloe Wicks. Level 1 childcare. 2nd year.	No.	Level 2 hairdressing.	Poor behaviour.	Safeguarding file held.		

Table 5.6 *Progression monitoring document (extract) with suggested actions.*

Learner name	Targets for improvement	Actions to be taken and notes
Lewis Parker	Attend all lessons from w/c 24.03 to w/c 07.04. (To be reviewed 11.04.)	One-to-one meeting to discuss attendance; set and agree targets and clarify current non-progression.
		Liaison with mental health support workers, teachers and parents to check awareness of support plan and necessary accommodation being made.
Amir Hassan	Attend all lessons from w/c 24.03 to w/c 07.04. (To be reviewed 11.04.)	One-to-one meeting to discuss attendance; set and agree targets and clarify current non-progression. Since there were some low-level ABC issues in first year, reinforce that there must be improvements in the remainder of the year for his application to be viewed favourably by the receiving curriculum area.
		Also, a one-to-one to discuss previous bullying situation and reinforce agreements and conditions on others after the mediation meeting held.
		Involvement of parents to discuss any continuing bullying concerns and choice of computing.
		Liaison with my manager, Steve, to approach receiving curriculum area's manager (Matt) regarding a possible meeting and any further actions he wants to see, for example a written application stating why he wants to do computing and how he thinks ABC will improve. I can support with this and also ask Steve to state to Matt that he could thrive in a new department with a different set of learners.
Chloe Wicks	Keep to agreed targets set in PLC meeting in term one. (To be reviewed Fri 11.04 in tutorial.)	With Chloe's teachers and aided by additional support staff, revisit strategies for working with Chloe (developed having read her safeguarding file in term one).
		One-to-one meeting to discuss behaviour and attitude; set and agree targets and clarify current non-progression. Reinforce understanding of the necessary standards.
	Receive positive comments on weekly report to commence w/c 24.03 and be reviewed Fri 11.04.	Copy of the above one-to-one meeting with agreed targets to Chloe's foster-mum (Karen) along with a phone call to emphasise next year will be Chloe's third year in college so improvements must be seen.
		Liaison with my manager Steve to approach receiving curriculum area's manager (Zainab) regarding a possible meeting and any further actions she wants to see, for example I can help to cascade teaching approaches developed this year for Chloe to the new team for next year. Also, I can support her with writing an application stating why she wants to do hairdressing and how she intends to improve her ABC.

External progression

External progression is about the destinations of your learners and your support in getting them there. Examples of external destinations are entering higher education, starting work or an apprenticeship.

The personal tutor's role in learner destinations

Critical thinking activity 5

» *You have two learners in one of your level 3 (second year) groups who want different destinations after college: Sima wants to go to university while Brad wants to go into work. List as many things as you can which you will do to prepare them for their external progression.*

Discussion

Compare your answers to those in Tables 5.7 and 5.8.

Table 5.7 *Some good practice in preparing Sima for university*

Actions for Sima to carry out	Aim	How we will cover these topics/ how I can support Sima in carrying out these actions
Start and complete the UCAS process including completion of personal statement.	Complete a strong university application.	• Introduction to UCAS process within group tutorial and careers adviser to speak in tutorial. • Group tutorial session(s) on personal statements. • Once process is underway – monitoring progress within one-to-one meetings with Sima in term two.
Research universities: • location; • courses (including schemes of assessment); • research graduate careers from chosen degree(s), including starting salaries.	Make an informed choice about which universities to apply to.	• Research methods and topics within group tutorial (in computer room). • Set targets for research topic completion within Sima's first one-to-one in term two.

Table 5.7 (*cont.*)

Actions for Sima to carry out	Aim	How we will cover these topics/ how I can support Sima in carrying out these actions
Undertake visits to universities. Outcomes from visits to be ranked in terms of: • location; • course (including assessment types and schedule); • employment prospects after course. Leading to an overall ranking of universities visited.	Make an informed choice about which universities to apply to.	• Give information about university visits that the college is doing as a whole. • Discuss Sima's individual choices and enable individual visits through discussing time management in one-to-ones in term one.
Assessment of: • financial situation; • money management; • budgeting.	Accurate assessment of financial burden of university to inform budgeting and paid work which may be necessary alongside university.	• Within group tutorials through a variety of learning activities. • Revisit in one-to-one meeting.
Five-year career plan.	University application to be informed by long-term career aim and plan.	• Introduce five-year career plan with whole group in group tutorial. • Set completion as a target within Sima's one-to-one meetings and check she has finished and updated these.

Table 5.8 *Some good practice in preparing Brad for work*

Actions for Brad to carry out	Aim	How we will cover these topics/how I can support Brad in carrying out these actions
Complete professional and comprehensive CV and personal statement (check, reformat and update current CV).	To have professional documents for job applications.	• Group tutorial on CV and personal statement writing. • Set target for completion of these in Brad's one-to-one in term one.

Table 5.8 (*cont.*)

Actions for Brad to carry out	Aim	How we will cover these topics/how I can support Brad in carrying out these actions
Self-assess employability skills and readiness for work and provide evidence for this.	Identify areas of strength and areas for development in terms of employability skills.	• Introduce and start 'checking how ready I am for work' resource in group tutorial. • Brad and other learners to use throughout the year to update ranking against each criterion. • Completion of 'employability profile' with evidence of skills and experience gained both in college and in work experience.
Have and practice good interview skills.	To be confident in how to approach interviews and have necessary interview skills.	• Mock interviews arranged in term one with local employers (through Mary in careers). • Verbal and written feedback on this to inform one-to-ones and further target setting.
Improve knowledge of time management strategies and put into practice.	Develop time management skills necessary for the world of work.	• Group tutorial on time management. • Time management revisited in Brad's one-to-one.
Research career pathways.	Gain a clear picture of common and realistic career pathways from course.	• Group tutorial and one-to-one time on career pathways. • Arrangement of guest speakers to come into group tutorial. • Help him phone employers to find out further information.
Go on work experience.	Gain relevant work experience.	• Signpost Brad to relevant team who can help find a suitable placement. • Help him reflect on lessons learned from work experience.

What about learners who are not progressing and need alternative provision?

When we talk about external progression and destinations we don't only mean university and employment. We also have a role to play regarding learners who need to find alternative provision away from the institution either in-year or at the end of the academic year (due to a variety of reasons including not being recommended to progress). Along with our sense of social responsibility, the government agenda to reduce the number of 'NEETs' (those not in education, employment or training) means you and the institution have a duty to not simply wave goodbye to these learners but to support these young people's progression, even if it is to another provider. Moreover, from an institutional perspective, Ofsted's focus is increasingly on these destinations.

Both supporting this external progression and knowing where learners have ended up (thus being able to provide destination data to the institution and inspectors) are made difficult by the nature of these learners; for example, they may be long-term absentees who have been uncontactable for some time.

Are you, as personal tutor, the sole person responsible for alternative external progression? Bearing in mind the expertise and temporal (time) boundaries, the answer is no. However, at times it may feel as though you are! The resourcing, in terms of staff, at the institutions you work in will vary. As a result, the extent of this responsibility will vary and others involved are, hopefully, likely to include careers advisers and support managers.

Working with learners who have additional support needs

There is plenty of information already out there on the topic of additional support needs themselves, in terms of the definitions, approaches, issues and support needs related to specific learning difficulties and disabilities. Rather, this section is concerned with your role as a personal tutor regarding your learners who have support needs and with other staff within the institution when it comes to these issues.

But first, a quick note on terminology. Some different terms are used within FE. Learners can be referred to as having learning difficulties and disabilities (LDD) or special educational needs and disability (SEND) or ASN (additional support needs). As you can see from the title of this section, we are using the last of these but without the acronym ASN. The staff employed to work directly with these learners may also have different titles. One of the most common for the relevant group of staff or department is 'additional support', which is the term we use.

Critical thinking activity 6

You have a learner, Duncan, who has an additional support need. We have not specified the particular support need on purpose since we want you to think about what your role is as a personal tutor in necessary processes for learners with additional support needs generally, rather than specific actions related to a particular need which can have a wide range of individual differences within them.

1. List what you think are the key actions to support Duncan generally.

2. For each action, state whether it should be carried out by you as personal tutor, other members of staff or a combination of both.

3. Make notes that explain and discuss how you decided on your answers to question 2 and how important each action is.

Table 5.9 *Additional support actions, roles and explanations*

Action	Who to carry out?	Explanation and discussion
With Duncan, complete a referral to the additional support department for assessment.	Any member of staff working with Duncan	This may have already happened at an early stage of the year and Duncan may have declared his need at enrolment, meaning an additional referral from you is not necessary. You may have other learners who you feel might benefit from additional support but who haven't had any referral, and who you'll need to refer.
Talk to Duncan in his first one-to-one meeting about support needs and whether he feels they are being met.	Personal tutor	This is an important part of your initial one-to-one and subsequent one-to-one meetings. It needs handling sensitively of course in that a learner may not want undue attention being drawn to the additional support need. Also, it has been declared but is confidential between the learner and relevant staff.
Adapt my approach in one-to-ones and group tutorial for Duncan.	Personal tutor	Like other teachers, your own approach to a learner such as Duncan in face-to-face support and learning situations may need adapting (as informed by an individual support plan).
Talk to Duncan's parents/guardians about his support needs.	Personal tutor	We need to remember that all learners are individual in terms of their particular support need and how they feel about it being discussed. Therefore, parents/guardians can be the best first port of call to get a clear picture of the support and also the best way to approach interactions with the learner.
Use information about Duncan's additional support needs to inform at risk meetings, documentation and actions.	Personal tutor	Continuing with the holistic view, these issues need to inform at-risk discussions and actions. Of course, Duncan may be judged to be 'no risk' or 'low risk' if there is no negative impact on his chances of success and appropriate support is in place.

Communicate with the relevant member of the additional support team.	Personal tutor and other staff	Clear communication and conversations are paramount. Other teaching staff should also be in regular communication with the relevant additional support staff, but as the primary support, there will be much with you.
Raise awareness of support need to the department and teachers.	Additional support staff; possibly the personal tutor	You can have a role in raising awareness of support needs and issues, particularly if you feel there is a need for this in the curriculum area. However, it is not your primary role on a formal level and additional support staff also need to be proactive in this.
Advise other teaching staff about how they need to adapt their teaching and approach to Duncan.	Additional support staff; possibly the personal tutor	While you can have a role in this, the relevant additional support member of staff is key here and this information should be on a shared individual support plan for a learner such as Duncan and, ideally, uploaded to the electronic learner tracking and monitoring system.
Work with in-class support for Duncan.	All teaching staff including the personal tutor	If allocated, these are members of staff you need to work with in group tutorials (and possibly one-to-ones).
Ensure additional support information informs any PLCs, and/or disciplinary meetings that Duncan may have. Ensure a relevant additional support member of staff is present in disciplinary meetings.	Personal tutor; relevant managers	This information should inform disciplinary meetings and it is good practice for a member of the additional support team to be present as another advocate for the learner in an appropriate way. The latter is not directly your role and the managers should initiate this; however, you can be useful in reminding those organising the meeting that this should happen.
Undergo training in Duncan's specific support need.	Possibly the personal tutor and other teaching staff	While most institutions will have specialist teachers and thus the 'experts', it is useful for personal tutors to undergo training in additional support needs and learning difficulties. It is not a prerequisite of working with a learner with a particular need, but in order to provide holistic support you may request this or research and talk to others informally.
Allocate support staff.	Additional support manager	It is not your role, but if you feel there's a need you can discuss the requirement for resourcing with your line manager or directly with the additional support manager.

Discussion

Compare your answers to the suggestions in Table 5.9.

To fulfil the aim of providing outstanding and holistic support to learners, additional support needs have to be taken into account. You are the primary support, but additional support staff are another key arm of this. As such, and as we have seen, additional support issues are something you will have much involvement with while at the same time remembering the expertise and temporal boundaries. You are not expected to be an expert in all of these needs, but you will inevitably gain more knowledge of these issues as you undertake the role and you may want to pursue an area of particular interest for your own development. A clear referral process, both internal and external, is key. Also, a connection is often needed between additional support and safeguarding, the topic of the final section of this chapter.

Safeguarding

Cast your mind back to the beginning of the book. There we listed all of the different roles you have to play, thinking of them in terms of alternative job titles. Among them was social worker. Once again, we need to remember the expertise boundary. You are not a social worker but a teacher. However, any social issues relating to a particular learner will almost certainly impact upon the things you are given the task of ensuring: effective learning and assessment; stretch and challenge; the retention of learners in the institution; and that their ABC is up to standard. Moreover, you are often the individual with whom learners build the most trusting relationship, meaning that they may often talk to you about such issues rather than speaking to other individuals either within or external to the institution.

You will no doubt be familiar with the term 'safeguarding'. 'To safeguard' has a generic definition of '*protect from harm or damage with an appropriate measure*' (Oxford Dictionaries, n.d., online) and the legislation regarding safeguarding is set out in the Children's Act of 2004. This definition tells us that it is the duty of all staff and the institution to safeguard *all* learners; but in the day-to-day language of the educational institution it is often used as an umbrella term for those learners who have had, or are still undergoing, safeguarding issues. The typical statement when discussing a learner may be 'she does have a safeguarding file'. Among the issues involved could be domestic violence, abuse, sexual exploitation or neglect.

Much information already exists on the topic of safeguarding. In this section, we want you to think about your role as a personal tutor in relation to this, rather than provide an in-depth study and exploration. Also, the number of safeguarding issues you encounter will depend on the make-up of the overall learner cohort in your institution.

In a scenario where a learner discloses information to you which suggests that they may be vulnerable to harm, it is simply a case of referring the information to the relevant staff at your institution – for example the 'safeguarding officers'. What we are talking about here is where safeguarding information is already held on a learner within your cohort. Ideally, this information informs your approach from the beginning of the academic year, but it can be received in-year. The processes at your institution should ensure that you are a member of staff with whom relevant safeguarding information is shared.

CASE STUDY

Supporting Emily

A support manager has received a safeguarding file about one of your learners, Emily, from the school she attended prior to college, and has suggested you read it. Below is an extract from a report in the file.

15 July
From Chris Wilkins, Head of Year 12, Shotley Park Secondary School

Emily was removed from the care of her birth parents at the age of nine. This was as a result of reported abuse and neglect. She has been in foster care since that time. There were behavioural problems at school resulting in an exclusion from her previous school. Emily has difficulty with authority figures and in taking responsibility for her actions. Emily's emotional state can be unpredictable and she can overreact to situations if feeling threatened or overly pressured. The educational psychologist's report suggested Emily has a younger emotional age than her 15 years nine months. Academically, Emily excels at certain focused tasks, more on the practical side. Socially, Emily can find it difficult to mix with new peers and tends to form separate groups, which can be with learners who are a 'bad influence'.

Critical thinking activity 7

Read the case study extract and then answer the following.

1. What are the key points for your role and how will it inform your support of Emily?

2. How do you think other members of staff should be involved and what would you tell other members of staff about?

Discussion

Safeguarding reports come in a mixture of formats. They can be divided up under topic headings or dates or as continuous writing, as in our example. They may stick to facts or make suggestions about approach. There is a need for you to pick out the key points, and it could be good practice to do this with a support manager.

Complex case

At first, it can be easy to be daunted by cases like Emily and not knowing where to start. However, you need to remember that all learners, whether they have complex backgrounds and needs or not, all react differently. There's also a need to not let such information unduly influence your view of an individual. Their past experiences may not adversely affect them in a new environment in which they may, hopefully, thrive. You need to avoid putting this in danger by 'overcompensating', and you should strike a balance between being aware of the issues, adapting your approach appropriately and seeing a learner like Emily with fresh eyes and giving her the same opportunity as any others.

Foster care

A good starting point would be to contact those who know her best, her foster parents, about support and approach.

Unpredictable emotional states

Communication with additional support is necessary. Receiving direct support relies on Emily's consent, but strategies such as a 'time out card' and 'cooling off period' would seem to be relevant here.

Difficulty with authority figures and taking responsibility

As we have seen, your positive approach is about the young person understanding and investing in the process of improvement rather than dictating this to them. With Emily, your one-to-ones or PLCs will be important in reinforcing this. Since you are up against a history of resistance, you should not get disheartened if progress is slow and change is incremental.

Academically, Emily excels at certain focused tasks

You need to reinforce the positive with Emily and link that to positive feelings and beliefs in one-to-one meetings and conversations. 'How can you do more of this?' is the key reinforcing question to use with Emily when emphasising these positives.

Involving other members of staff

There is not a need to give the specific background details to other staff who teach Emily, for example the details of the abuse suffered. As we have seen though, you can take an advisory role for other teachers regarding teaching and group strategies for Emily and adapting your own group tutorial in a similar way. Additional support staff can aid her. There is a similarity to the additional support issues of the last section: considered communication is every-thing. Action plans can be drawn up, with additional support and possibly involving yourself, and ideally kept on the electronic learner tracking and monitoring system. This can, in turn, inform disciplinary meetings (where it is not to be used as an *excuse* for poor behaviour but rather to inform and be taken into account).

A final thought on safeguarding

Finally, these can be emotionally draining issues and you need to make sure you look after yourself. Structured offloading, where you talk about your most complex cases, can be very important in reducing the likelihood of taking your worries about these issues home with you, and to reassure you that you are doing the right things and all that you can.

Summary

The personal tutor role can feel all-encompassing, and a dizzying feeling can come from the sense that almost everything in your institution is of relevance to it. Moreover, when we start, not only do we not necessarily know the answers to the questions but we may not know what questions to ask in the first place! This chapter has, hopefully, addressed both of these issues by informing you:

- which the key procedures for the personal tutor are;
- what the procedures are and a good practice model for each;
- how you and others need to operate within the procedures most effectively.

Moreover, you should now have the terminology in order to further understand and enquire about how things work in your institution.

If you want to be outstanding in the role and have ambitions to progress, you need to be a constructive enquirer of those around you including those in more senior roles. You'll need the appropriate knowledge and language to do this. There will be more on the higher-level support skills to become outstanding in the next five chapters where we also discuss the bigger picture enquiries needed when you're aiming to be outstanding.

Learning checklist

Tick off each point when you feel confident you understand it.

- ☐ *I know how a policy and a procedure relate to each other and also the difference between them.*

- ☐ *I can identify the key institutional procedures for myself as personal tutor.*

- ☐ *I understand and can apply the tools to re-engage a learner in order to effect behavioural change without using punitive measures.*

- ☐ *I recognise the necessity for learners to be on the right course from a learner, personal tutor, departmental and institutional perspective. I understand and can apply the principles of an effective right course review conversation with my learners.*

- ☐ *I understand that offering clear pathways to learners and achieving high levels of internal progression is desirable and I can explain the key points of an effective internal progression process.*

- ☐ *I recognise the importance of my role in ensuring appropriate destinations for my learners and I know the key support actions to take whether their intended route is, for example, entering higher education, employment or an apprenticeship.*

- ☐ *I understand my role with learners in my cohort who have additional support needs. I understand what actions I can take for these learners and the role of other staff within the institution when it comes to these issues.*

☐ *I recognise that a variety of safeguarding issues relating to any of my learners can impact upon their overall performance.*

☐ *I understand how to read and analyse safeguarding reports and am able to draw out the key points to inform my own support actions. I know the role of others within the institution when it comes to these issues.*

Critical reflections

1. How much knowledge do you have of these key procedures from your teacher training course?

2. To what extent do you know the procedures in your institution most relevant to you and your role within them as personal tutor? If this is limited, using the knowledge gained from this chapter, can you find out yourself and who do you need to ask?

3. Can you recognise in your institution the key procedures discussed in this chapter? Do you think your institution has all of these procedures? Are there additional ones? Are there different titles and is alternative terminology used?

4. To what extent do you think procedures and the roles of staff within them are known and communicated in your institution? If limited, how can this be improved?

Personal tutor self-assessment system

The key procedures for the personal tutor are:

- disciplinary – a positive approach;
- right course review;
- internal progression;
- external progression;
- working with learners who have additional support needs;
- safeguarding.

PERSONAL TUTOR SELF-ASSESSMENT SYSTEM: *Chapter 5 the learner experience – key procedures*

	Minimum standard 2 points	Bronze 4 points	Silver 6 points	Gold 8 points	Platinum 10 points
Individual	I am aware of the key procedures from first meetings with my line manager and have a general understanding of them. I have some involvement with the procedures and how they relate to them.	I have a clear understanding of the content of the key procedures and how they work. This informs my support actions for relevant learners at an individual and group level.	I communicate with other staff about the key procedures. I have a clear understanding of my role and others within them (and know when it needs to be a combined approach).	My actions within the key procedures put the learner first and provide holistic and comprehensive support.	I reflect and constructively question key procedures with managers and others involved to review and improve them regularly. This is a significant factor in improving some key performance indicators.
Institutional	My institution has the key procedures in place and staff are generally aware of them.	The key procedures are effectively communicated to all new staff and updates for existing staff are frequent.	All staff clearly know their role within the key procedures and carry these out effectively. This is a significant factor in the retention of learners.	Managers ensure the key procedures embody a holistic approach to all relevant learners. This contributes to the improvement of some key performance indicators.	The key procedures are regularly reviewed by involving all relevant learner-facing staff and a selection of learners. As a result, staff feel invested in them. There is a highly consistent approach to the key procedures across my institution.

The self-assessment system is available as a free download from the publisher's website and the authors' websites (all listed at the start of the book).

Taking it further

Related to right course review:

Fuller, C and Macfayden, T (2012) 'What, With Your Grades?' Students' Motivation for and Experiences of Vocational Courses in Further Education, *Journal of Vocational Education and Training*, 64 (1): 87–101.

Related to external progression, in particular for definitions and approaches to NEETs:

Department for Children, Schools and Families (2008), *NEET Toolkit: Reducing the Proportion of Young People Not in Education, Employment or Training (NEET)*. Nottingham: DCSF Publications.

Nelson, J and O'Donnell, L (2012) *Approaches to Supporting Young People Not in Education, Employment or Training: a Review (NFER Research Programme: From Education to Employment)*. Slough: NFER.

Public Health England (2014), *Local Action on Health Inequalities: Reducing the Number of Young People Not in Employment, Education or Training (NEET). Health Equity Evidence Review 3*. London: PHE Publications.

Related to additional support:

www.gov.uk/schools-colleges-childrens-services/special-educational-needs-disabilities.

Related to safeguarding:

Department for Education (2015) *Keeping Children Safe in Education: Statutory Guidance for Schools and Colleges*. Dfes.

A useful safeguarding self-assessment tool for institutions: www.esat.nspcc.org.uk.

Ofsted (2011) *Best Practice in Safeguarding in Colleges: A Survey of Best Practice in Safeguarding Based on Visits to 14 of the 15 Colleges That Received an Outstanding Grade for the Leadership and Management of their Safeguarding Arrangements in 2009/10*. Manchester: Ofsted.

References

Cotton, D (2010) The effect structured listening and learning has on pupils and schools following incidents involving physical intervention. [online] Available at: www.academia.edu/5138877/ The_Effect_structured_listening_and_learning_has_on_pupils_and_schools_following_ incidents_involving_physical_intervention._2010b [accessed May 2015].

Cotton, D (2013a) What is the impact of implementing an IT based post-incident learning APP as an alternative to after school detentions in a mainstream secondary school? [online] Available at: www.academia.edu/5138880/What_is_the_impact_of_implementing_an_IT_based_PIL_ APP_as_an_alternative_to_detentions_2013 [accessed May 2015].

Cotton, D (2013b) PIL Presentation. [online] Available at www.academia.edu/5138876/PIL_ Presentation [accessed May 2015].

Development Agency www.oxforddictionaries.com (n.d.) [online]. Term searched for: 'to safeguard'. [accessed May 2014].

Fuller, C and Macfayden, T (2012) cited in Wallace, S (2013) When You're Smiling: Exploring How Teachers Motivate and Engage Learners in the Further Education Sector. *Journal of Further and Higher Education*, 38 (3): 346–60.

Martinez, P (2001) *Improving Student Retention and Achievement: What Do We Know and What do We Need to Find Out? LSDA report*. London: Learning and Skills.

Wallace, S (2013a) When You're Smiling: Exploring How Teachers Motivate and Engage Learners in the Further Education sector. *Journal of Further and Higher Education*. 38 (3): 346–60.

Wallace, S (2013b) *Understanding the Further Education Sector: A Critical Guide to Policies and Practices*. Northwich: Critical Publishing.

6 Using solution-focused coaching with learners

Chapter aims

This chapter helps you to:

- understand solution-focused coaching and the solution-focused approach;

- consider the key characteristics of using a solution-focused approach in your personal tutoring role;

- explore how solution talk and problem talk questions can impact upon learners;

- examine the phases within the OSKAR framework in relation to conversations with learners.

Introduction

The previous chapters have concentrated on the 'essentials' of the personal tutor role. This chapter and the following ones are aimed at improving your higher-level skills to enable you to work towards becoming an outstanding personal tutor.

This chapter explores the use of solution-focused coaching techniques and tools and explains how, by employing some or all of these in your day-to-day conversations with learners, you can encourage them to aim higher, achieve outcomes faster, explore barriers to learning more positively and, more importantly, help them to find their own solutions. One of the principal features of a solution-focused coaching approach, and one of the reasons why we advocate its use with learners through your personal tutor role, is that it can significantly reduce any inferiority learners feel about themselves or their current situation. Furthermore, in terms of emotional well-being, experience shows that this approach helps learners to think more optimistically, behave more confidently, and engage with their goals, which become more self-generated.

The solution-focused approach grew out of techniques from the world of therapy in America in the 1980s. Solution-focused brief therapy was developed by American social workers Steve De Shazer, Insoo Kim Berg and their team at the Milwaukee Brief Family Therapy Center. Through their practice and research, they discovered that their clients made much greater progress over a shorter period of time when the conversations focused more on the clients' future goals, a positive view of the future, and on their own strengths and competencies. From these early days, the solution-focused approach has grown and is now used successfully in a variety of settings, such as business consulting, hypnotherapy, counselling and coaching within the commercial world, as well as in education.

What is solution-focused coaching?

There are many definitions of coaching but one of the most widely recognised is: '*coaching is unlocking a person's potential to maximise their own performance. It is helping them to learn rather than teaching them*' (Whitmore, 2002). The solution-focused approach to coaching is, as the title suggests, essentially trying to make greater progress with the learner by focusing on where they want to get to and understanding what skills and knowledge they need to get there, rather than spending excessive amounts of time exploring the problem or issue they may be facing.

Solution-focused coaching has links with cognitive behavioural therapy (CBT), which has also led to the development of another strand of coaching called cognitive behavioural coaching (CBC). CBT and CBC are similar, but CBC focuses on achieving personal and professional fulfilment, not an understanding of psychological disturbance, which is a core component of CBT (Neenan, 2009). CBC and solution-focused coaching are also similar; however, CBC is a fusion of cognitive behavioural therapy, rational emotive therapy, solution-focused approaches, goal-setting theory and social cognitive theory (Palmer and Szymanska, 2008). Even though there are similarities between solution-focused coaching and cognitive behavioural therapy, the main difference is that solution-focused coaching primarily focuses on goal achievement rather than healing.

Put simply, there are two different approaches that you can adopt when helping learners to solve their problems, as illustrated in Table 6.1. While both can work well, the solution-focused approach enables greater self-efficacy and self-reliance leading towards more self-directed, independent learning and learners (all of which are highly desirable outcomes for your personal tutor role and the educational institution).

Table 6.1 *Different approaches to helping learners solve their problems* (Adapted from Jackson and McKergow, 2007)

Problem-focus approach	Solution-focus approach
Understand and diagnose the problem.	Recognise what solution or outcome the learner would find desirable or is needed.
Know what causes the problem.	Find know-how and resources; in other words, skills or previous experience, which will help the learner to work towards the solution or agreed outcome.
Use this information to address and fix the problem.	Taking into account the learner's know-how, explore the solution and agree a small action, or actions and often the problem that the learner was facing will either reduce or seem less significant to them and together you may discover a new way to overcome it.

There are a number of factors that can influence the effectiveness of both approaches such as:

- the focus or desired outcome of the conversation;

- the degree of rapport and depth of relationship you have with the learner;

- how much time you have for the conversation;

- the level of motivation and emotional intelligence that the learner possesses.

Key characteristics of using solution-focused coaching with learners

Table 6.2 illustrates some of the key characteristics that will help focus the way you view and use solution-focused coaching in your day-to-day conversations with learners and in your personal tutor role.

Table 6.2 *Key characteristics of using solution-focused coaching with learners*

Key characteristic	Explanation
Positive change can occur.	Solution-focused coaching works on the assumption that positive change can occur with learners and that this change can happen quickly.
Clear goals and self-directed action.	You should work with the learners to define specific goals. A good coaching conversation doesn't stop when it stops. Set a clear expectation that the learners must be self-directed and take the responsibility to implement actions to achieve these goals outside the coaching conversations.

Table 6.1 (*cont.*)

Key characteristic	Explanation
Develop solutions and focus on the future; not dwelling on problems within the past or present.	Listen to any issues or problems in order to communicate empathy and develop rapport with your learners. Quickly move the conversation on to exploring future goals, past successes, and what skills, knowledge and abilities they have.
Learners' experience, expertise and resources.	A solution-focused personal tutor is an enabler and facilitator. There is a belief that learners are likely to already have the answers and the ability to take themselves forward, and as their personal tutor it is your role to help them notice this. When learners feel they have worked something out for themselves, there is a greater chance that they will ask themselves the same questions in the future and coach themselves. The best coaches in some ways become invisible.
Reframe the learners' perspective and help them to notice positives.	Possibilities include reframing and helping them to notice: • a distant possibility as a near possibility; • a weakness as a strength; • a problem as an opportunity.

Reframing

Reframing learners' perspectives isn't always an easy task, particularly if they have a negative belief about themselves or their situation, but experience has shown that it is an effective tool and one that you can hone with practice. The new framing of their perspective needs to be felt, or in other words it usually needs to have an emotional impact and be more emotionally compelling than their old view. Try using the phrase 'Let's look at it another way' and encourage them to stand in the other frame by exploring it through dialogue, to give them the best chance to really see it. Sometimes the learner might not be in the right frame of mind to have the view 'reframed'. A receptive mood is usually necessary, otherwise the effort may be wasted.

Reframing can affect learners' emotional state, hopefully making them happier, more positive and optimistic. Negative emotions from learners are not always detrimental to their academic progress. However, research studies, particularly in the fields of positive psychology and neuroscience, and summarised by Felicia Huppert (Department of Psychiatry, University of Cambridge, 2006) suggest that people who have more positive emotions or are more regularly in a positive mood tend to:

• engage with goal pursuits that are more self-generated and consistent with personal values;

• have a broader focus of attention; in other words they can see the 'bigger picture';

• generate more ideas in problem-solving tasks;

- build enduring coping resources, which leads to resilience;

- evaluate themselves and others more positively.

Helping learners to notice

We have found that one of the main ways of understanding when learners finally notice something new about themselves or their situation can be seen in their facial expressions. We call this the 'lightbulb moment' and it may only be evident through the appearance of a tiny new smile or an expression that says, 'Ah, now I get it!' The best way to enable learners to really notice something about themselves is through careful and considered questioning, rather than telling them what they should notice. *Telling* learners can work, but enabling *them* to notice crucial aspects of themselves or their situation, in other words raising their self-awareness, is key as this helps to develop more enduring ownership of their situation and self-reliance, which in turn promotes greater self-efficacy.

CASE STUDY

Luke and Simon

The following dialogue is taken from a discussion between Luke, who is studying level 3 computing, and his personal tutor and teacher, Simon.

LUKE: *Could I have a chat with you?*

SIMON: *Yes sure, grab a seat.*

LUKE: *I'm sorry that I haven't been to all of your classes lately, I've had a few things on.*

SIMON: *Okay, do you want tell me about it?*

LUKE: *Well... If I'm honest, I've kind of lost a bit of motivation for the course, which I know isn't what you want to hear. I actually do want to study computing at university but I've been doing a lot more hours at my part-time job and I've been thinking about whether I should leave and work full-time.*

SIMON: *I've been there when I was at college, so I know quite a bit about what you're thinking about.*

LUKE: *Really?*

SIMON: *Yes, I remember when I was at college, I didn't know whether I should carry on or try and get a job and earn some money. I had a part-time job like you in an evening, which was good for the money but didn't really help with my college work. I made the decision to do just enough hours to make sure I had enough money to attend college and for living the life that I wanted at the time. What I would do is reduce your hours to the point where you can earn just enough money to be able to do the things you want, and that way you can still continue with your course. I see this every year from students, it's nothing new.*

LUKE: *Okay.*

SIMON: *You are a capable student and I've seen some examples of really good work at times. In terms of your motivation for the course, do you actually want to continue?*

LUKE: *Yes, I think so… as I said, I'd actually love to go to uni to study computing.*

SIMON: *What I suggest you do then is what I did when I thought I didn't want to continue at college. Take a look at the career prospects for the job you are doing now. If you were doing it full-time, do you think you would want to be doing that job in three years' time?*

LUKE: *That's an easy one to answer, no I don't. Maybe what you've said is right, I might consider speaking to my boss to reduce my hours and try to focus more on my college work to be able to get to uni.*

Luke and Simon, take two

(we have omitted the first part of the dialogue to avoid repetition)

SIMON: *You are a capable student and I've seen some examples of really good work at times. In terms of your motivation for the course, do you actually want to continue?*

LUKE: *Yes, I think so… as I said I'd actually love to go to uni to study computing.*

SIMON: *Okay, suppose you achieve your ideal outcome, what would that look like?*

LUKE: *Erm, well, I think it would be me getting my motivation back and doing well on this course, so that I can get into the uni that I want.*

SIMON: *That seems clear. So, if on a scale of one to ten, where ten is you have achieved all this and one is where you have not achieved your ideal outcome at all and you have no idea how to do it, where are you now?*

LUKE: *I'd say probably about five, I guess.*

SIMON: *Five? That's really good. Okay, when have you overcome a situation like this before?*

LUKE: *…Well, now you mention it, I actually had this same issue at school. I totally lost my motivation to revise for my GCSEs, but I eventually got it back and did quite well in the end.*

SIMON: *Excellent! How did you manage that?*

LUKE: *Well, thinking back, I remember I actually did two things. I looked on the internet at what type of jobs I really wanted in the future and looked at the types of courses I could do to get there, which helped. I also did something I don't do very often, I talked to my mum and dad about it. They both work in IT and really enjoy their jobs.*

SIMON: *Okay, that sound great. So you said you feel you're at five on the scale, what made you be that high up the scale?*

LUKE: *...I suppose I don't normally like to give up on something or feel that I'm beaten. I've always been like that in the past, particularly when playing sport, like football.*

SIMON: *Okay, so if there was an expert on these issues here right now, what advice would they give you about tackling this?*

LUKE: *Well, I suppose they'd probably say to focus more on my college studies as that's what's going to get me to where I want to be in the future and think less about making a few extra quid right now, when I could cope without it.*

SIMON: *Right okay, sounds sensible. So, what are the next small steps that will start to help you achieve that goal, or let's put it another way, what's going to get you up to 5.1 on your scale?*

LUKE: *The first thing I need to do is speak to my boss at work and tell him I need to reduce my hours so I can concentrate on my college work.*

Critical thinking activity 1

In relation to versions one and two, note down your answers to the following questions:

1. In your view, which of these two conversations would be most useful to the learner and why?

2. What were the differences between them?

3. What went well in them?

Discussion

You may think, quite rightly, that version one shows a highly knowledgeable personal tutor, who clearly has his heart in the right place. On the face of it, Simon is doing a professional job by providing sensible advice to help Luke. However, Simon is more effective in version two because Luke seemingly arrives at the solution by himself, and this makes it more likely that he will believe he has the know-how and resources to achieve it. In reality, the solution has been co-created through solution-focused questioning.

Another important aspect to consider is the length of time you allow for the learner to answer your questions. A solution-focused approach is where the personal tutor lets silence 'do the heavy lifting', in other words, allowing for adequate thinking time and avoiding the temptation to jump in with your own answers. Following on from this, you should try to listen with solution-focused ears. For example, notice the learner's resources, skills and know-how.

Solution talk and problem talk

Solution talk is where you focus on discussing:

- what the learner wants to achieve or overcome;
- what is already working well for them;
- where else they are making progress;
- what resources and strengths they have;
- who else might be able to help them;
- possible solutions;
- actions the learner will take.

One example of solution talk among the many you may have noticed in version two of the case study is where Simon asks Luke, *'Five? That's really good. Okay, when have you overcome a situation like this before?'*

However, problem talk focuses on discussing:

- what is wrong or what issue the learner is facing;
- what the learner needs to fix;
- who is to blame for the issue;
- who has control over the problem or issue;
- what weaknesses or deficits need to be reduced or overcome;
- whether there is an expert who could help;
- what complications the learner might face.

In version one of the case study Simon didn't really use much problem talk; however, one thing he did excessively, which I'm sure you will have noticed, is that he set himself up as the expert, predominantly telling Luke what to do, instead of helping him to find the solution for himself and promote the essential attribute of self-efficacy in Luke. Offering advice and guidance as a personal tutor is required on occasion. However, wherever there is an acceptable opportunity to help learners to find the way forward on their own, we advise you to take it. If you don't coach within your personal tutor role there is a danger that learners will see you as the source of all information; coaching actually makes your job easier and your learners more self-directed and effective.

Since you need to recognise the temporal (time) boundary, we advocate placing greater emphasis on solution talk because experience has shown that it can be a more effective use of the finite time you have. This is not to suggest that you don't let the learner explain any issues they are experiencing; you should allow learners to explain what's happening in their lives and how it makes them feel; but you should always try to spend more of your time on solution talk rather than problem talk as this is more likely to enable the learners to make greater progress and save time for you in the long term.

You should consider the impact of the language you use on the way you want your learners to feel. You may already use more solution talk when working with learners and this is likely to make them feel more optimistic and motivated about the improvements or changes you want them to make. Equally, problem talk questions can have a strong impact and be effective in some situations, for example when you are trying to reprimand a learner. Table 6.3 provides some examples of both types of questions.

Table 6.3 *Potential solution talk and problem talk questions*

Reproduced with permission, Lincoln (2004)

Solution talk questions	Problem talk questions
How did you know how to do that?	Why did you do that?
What might you do differently?	What should you have done?
What have you done before that worked?	Have you done that before?
What did you do to contribute to the outcome?	Is there anything you did that helped?
What could you do to ensure this happens?	What are the obstacles to you achieving this?
How can you make sure this happens again?	Why can't you do that more often?
What was the best you have ever done at this?	What's the main cause of your difficulty?
What else?	Anything else?

Table 6.4 *Problem talk and solution talk questions*

(Jackson and McKergow, 2004)

Problem talk questions	Solution talk questions
What's wrong with what you're doing?	What are you aiming to achieve?
Why are you doing so badly?	How will you know you've achieved it?
What's the main cause of your difficulty?	What was the best you have ever done at this?
Whose fault is it?	What went well on that occasion?
What are the other things that make it hard?	What will be the first signs that you are getting better?
Why will it be difficult for you to do any better?	How will other people notice this improvement?

Critical thinking activity 2

1. Think of one recent standout moment in your personal tutor role which didn't go to plan and which you would have liked to improve or change. With a trusted colleague, friend or family member, explain the standout moment to them in as much detail as possible.

2. A slightly different set of problem and solution talk questions is provided by Jackson and McKergow (2004) in Table 6.4.

    a. Get your work partner to ask you the problem talk questions in Table 6.4 and try to answer them.

    b. Then get them to ask you the solution talk questions from the same table and again try to answer them.

    c. What was different about being asked the first and the second set of questions?

    d. How were your feelings about your standout moment affected by the different question types?

    e. Which of the two types of questions are most likely to help motivate your learners to overcome problems or to achieve stretching goals and why?

The OSKAR framework

OSKAR is a framework for structuring solution-focused coaching conversations with learners. It is an acronym which stands for the main headings: Outcome, Scaling, Know-how, Affirm and action, Review (see below). It was created by Paul Jackson and Mark McKergow and is explained in their book, *The Solutions Focus: Making Coaching and Change SIMPLE* (2007).

*   **Outcome**: this is similar but subtly different to the goal in most coaching models. The outcome is not simply the goal of the coachee; it is the difference that the coachee (and those around the coachee) want to see as a result of the coaching.

*   **Scaling**: this enables you to find out what's working. You can ask learners to rate themselves on a scale from one to ten, where the desired outcome is ten and one is the complete opposite.

*   **Know-how and resources**: this phase focuses on finding out all about what works or what has worked for a learner, rather than what won't work or what is wrong. During the discussion you are able to establish what is already helping to make the learner, for example, four on the scale and not lower than that. A simple but useful question for you to use here is, 'What else?' This will allow you to build up a collection of what is already helping.

*   **Affirm and action**:

    o   this is where you affirm the positive qualities of the learner based on what you have heard during the conversation or what you have observed previously.

This helps to build the learner's self-belief and strengthens the relationship between you and the learner;

○ your solution-focused coaching should always end in an action. Try to find some small next steps to build on what is already working so that the learners can start or make progress towards their outcome. We've found with learners that either one or a number of small actions is enough for them to start making progress and to build their confidence. Express the small steps by asking what they can do to move themselves from 4 to 4.1 or 5 on their scale.

• **Review**: in either the arranged or opportune follow-up discussions, try to find out what's working and build on that. Useful phrases to use are 'what's better?' or 'what helped?' Focus predominantly on things that are helping the learners to move in the right direction and less on whether previous actions were carried out or what happened.

Each of the sections can be used together to structure a comprehensive coaching conversation or, if needed, they can be used in isolation or in groups of two, three or four sections.

It is a matter of personal choice whether you wish to use a framework; we advocate it because experience has shown that it can be useful to have a logical sequence for structuring the coaching conversations with learners in order to maintain a clear focus and avoid 'conversational drift'.

There are other frameworks, for example John Whitmore's (2002) GROW (which is typically a quicker framework to use), CLEAR (Hawkins and Smith, 2006) and PRACTICE (Palmer, 2007) among others, which arguably might be equally effective for structuring solution-focused conversations with learners. The key point to remember is to choose whichever framework suits you and your learners best and to focus on practising and perfecting your coaching skills.

Scaling

The tool of scaling is a useful aid and can be used in coaching conversations as well as a variety of other situations, but it is particularly effective for conversations on target setting, behaviour, motivation and assessing a learner's commitment to an action. Allowing learners to place a number on how they perceive, for example, their behaviour, ensures that they have thought about what has happened in comparison to previous experiences. This self-reflection allows them to focus on their current situation and provides you and them with an agreed and established platform to co-construct desired future improvements.

The use of scaling with numbers isn't always suitable, particularly with issues relating to difficult emotions. If this is the situation, you could try replacing the number scale with polar adjectives, for example, words including and between *strong* and *weak*, *happy* and *sad*, *high* and *low*, *adequate* and *inadequate*, or even the gesture of a *thumbs up* or *down* (or *in-between*). Our experience has shown that, particularly with quiet, shy learners or even those who don't like to chat or feel 'too cool' to talk (you will know the ones we mean), asking them to place themselves on a scale can really help to open up and kick-start the conversation.

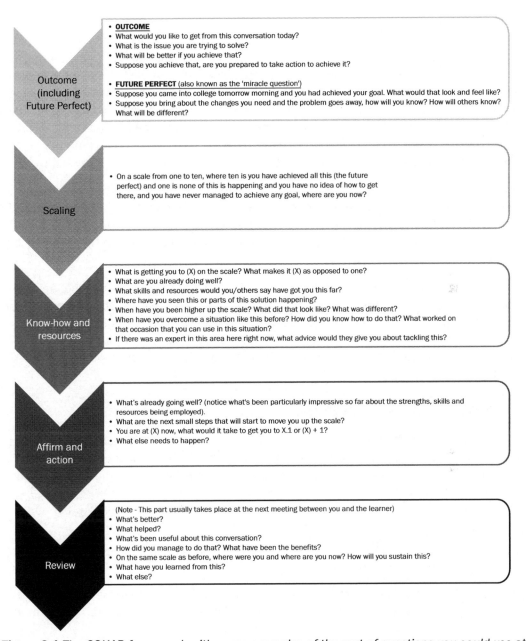

Figure 6.1 *The OSKAR framework with some examples of the sort of questions you could use at each stage (reproduced with permission, Lincoln, 2012)*

Other tips include adding humour to the learner being number one on the scale, for example by using extremes, such as number one being something really far-fetched. This can help to build rapport and make number ten seem more achievable. By doing this it often means the learners will rate themselves higher than one. If learners do place themselves low on the scale you could bring in positive emphasis and humour, for example 'Two, wow, double one!', in order for the learners to view their situation more positively.

Using OSKAR in practice

When you are trying to establish, for example, the desired outcome(s) with your learners, they may not be immediately obvious and you may need to revisit the idea throughout the conversation, which is okay and the right thing to do. If the nature of the conversation requires you to move forwards, backwards and around the sections of the OSKAR framework, then again this is okay as long as it feels useful for the learner. Furthermore, there is no set time for you to spend in each section; therefore try to allow the conversation to flow as naturally as possible, while bearing in mind the overall length of time you and the learner have for it.

Don't rush the platform (outcome and future perfect) because this is the foundation for everything that follows and, if possible, should account for approximately 50 per cent of the conversation. One way of thinking about this is like a train journey. You wouldn't step on the first train you see and hope that it will get you to your desired destination. You would establish where you want to end up first.

Another thing to consider is ways in which you can pull the learners away from the topic being discussed, to give them a bird's-eye or helicopter view of the situation. This can make them see it differently and more objectively. One way to do this could be to de-personalise the conversation by saying 'how would Luke know when things are going well?', in other words don't use 'you' but use the learner's name. This may enable them to notice what other people might see.

Critical thinking activity 3

» *Write a fictional dialogue using the OSKAR framework. Use a selection of some or all of the solution-focused tools and questions for a typical personal tutoring situation (it is also okay to use your own real examples). The fictional dialogue should end with a successful way forward for the learner being coached. Before starting to write, picture one of your current or previous learners for whom the context would apply. Potential examples include the following. A learner:*

- *wants to work towards achieving higher grades to be able to get into the university that they want;*

- *explains that they are struggling to meet assignment deadlines. You believe that this is because they are spending too much time with their new girlfriend or boyfriend;*

- *recognises that they don't display good behaviour in class but also realises that they need to improve.*

Discussion

Creating fictional dialogues is not easy. Hopefully, you will have thought about and included typical reactions and responses that you receive from your learners as well as considered your own natural questions and language. This activity, as well as continuing to reflect on your real-life coaching conversations, will help you to think through the different ways in which you can structure your solution talk as well as analyse what type of questions you may use in the future. We recommend that alongside using reflective practice to improve your skills, you continue to write solution-focused dialogues on real issues you are facing, as well as discussing these with trusted colleagues (remember to anonymise the learner's name) to jointly develop practice.

Critical thinking activity 4

1.   Which tool or aspect of solution-focused coaching or the OSKAR framework do you consider to be potentially the most useful for your own personal tutoring practice and why?

2.   In your next five one-to-one conversations with your learners, use a solution-focused approach and structure your conversation using the OSKAR framework. After each one, reflect on how it went and write down what was better and what more you would like to improve (read Chapter 8 to explore a number of reflective practice models).

A final thought

One final idea to consider is, if all of these tools and techniques could benefit learners then could they also be used to coach staff and even yourself? In short, the answer to both is yes; however, again, practice and reflection are key to increasing your effectiveness. Start with your learners and then, when you are comfortable with this, move on to applying the successful techniques in a wider context.

Summary

You should view the tools, techniques and framework within this chapter as part of your ever-increasing toolkit with which you can develop yourself to become an outstanding personal tutor. They aren't the 'magic wand' that will fix all of the issues you want to address or the areas you or your institution wish to improve. However, they are effective practical tools that you can use to help remove barriers to learning and to stretch, challenge and motivate your learners in the many and varied situations in which you work with them.

The coaching conversations you have with learners will not always go perfectly or have the perfect outcome, but practising the tools and techniques from this chapter is key to understanding which you prefer and feel comfortable with and in which contexts you feel they are and aren't appropriate. You should not get disheartened. Remember, the first few times you use solution-focused coaching, it can feel difficult and 'clunky', akin to learning to drive. Undertaking reflective practice (Chapter 8) regularly is important to identify what is and isn't working, and equally interlinked with this is asking your learners for feedback. Asking learners for genuine feedback on your coaching conversations is not something to be done lightly, however. Learners are not all skilled at offering feedback in a positive way. On occasions, we have seen experienced personal tutors and teachers receive soul-crushing feedback guaranteed to knock the confidence of the most battle-hardened classroom practitioner if it isn't done in a considered manner. In contrast though, when it is done well, we have seen learners offer up really insightful comments and motivational feedback which has made tutors feel truly appreciated and valued. If you wish to experiment with this, start small and do so on a one-to-one basis rather than with a whole class in the first instance.

Learning checklist

Tick off each point when you feel confident you understand it.

☐ *I understand that the primary focus of solution-focused coaching conversations with learners is to help co-construct effective solutions or improvements which leads to a greater chance of learners developing self-efficacy and taking ownership of their 'next steps'.*

☐ *I appreciate that the solution-focused approach and questions help to reduce any inferiority a learner may feel about their situation and improve their optimism.*

☐ *I recognise that reframing a learner's perspective can affect their emotional state, hopefully making them happier, more positive and optimistic.*

☐ *I can identify the tools of solution-focused coaching and understand that these and the sections of the OSKAR framework can be used in isolation, in groups or as a whole.*

☐ *I recognise that in order to become outstanding in using these tools I will need to practise and reflect regularly. Also, jointly sharing practice with colleagues will further develop my personal tutoring practice.*

☐ *I recognise that the tools and techniques from this chapter will benefit my learners; however, they could also be used to coach my colleagues and even myself.*

Critical reflections

1. To what extent do you feel you are already using a solution-focused approach and similar tools or approaches with your learners before reading this chapter?

2. Considering your experiences so far, explain the situations when you feel the solution-focused approach and OSKAR framework would be:

   a. most useful and effective;

   b. less useful and effective.

3. To what extent do you feel that the solution-focused approach fits within the culture, policies and aims of your current institution (if you have taught in more than one institution, use examples to compare and contrast the most recent two).

4. ***Schools must do more to tackle the root causes of bad behaviour, a leading children's charity has warned.***

   Barnardo's says unruly children may have special needs or serious problems at home. These may be causing them to 'act out' rather than 'act up' in class.

The government's behaviour tsar Charlie Taylor has said there has been an increase in children who need more help and support to tackle their problems. He added that these groups needed 'extra interventions' and 'more help' and for whom the 'basic standards of just a really well-run school aren't enough'. He has also called for all trainee teachers to be equipped with adequate behaviour management training.

Barnardo's chief executive Anne Marie Carrie said: 'A school teacher's job is not an easy one, but they must look behind the behaviour to see the child. The charity argues that behavioural problems often start at home or in the community, with some youngsters dealing with issues such as domestic violence or parents who are drug addicts.

(British Broadcasting Corporation, 2012, online)

In your view, how might the solution-focused approach, tools, techniques and the OSKAR framework help to address or mitigate some of the behavioural issues you face?

5. If you find that the tools and techniques from this chapter improve your skills, your performance and your effectiveness as a personal tutor, what could you do to increase their use with the following?

    a. Other staff within your institution.

    b. Other trainees on your teaching training course.

Personal tutor self-assessment system

See following table.

PERSONAL TUTOR SELF-ASSESSMENT SYSTEM: Chapter 6 using solution-focused coaching with learners

	Minimum standard 2 points	Bronze 4 points	Silver 6 points	Gold 8 points	Platinum 10 points
Individual	I use open and positively phrased questions to encourage my learners to define clear goals and think for themselves. I encourage them to think about what experience, expertise and resources they have to achieve their goals.	I regularly practise the use of solution talk style questions (where appropriate) to support my learners.	I regularly receive positive feedback on the impact that my learners feel my coaching conversations have on their progress.	I use reflective practice regularly to explore and improve my coaching practice. I regularly use the OSKAR framework (or other) to structure my coaching conversations with learners.	I measure the impact of my coaching conversations. I share my experiences of the solution-focused approach and OSKAR framework (or other) with my colleagues and am regularly involved in joint practice development activities to explore new ways to support learners through coaching conversations.
Institutional	The culture and policies of my institution clearly encourage all staff to take a positive approach towards learners and the issues or problems they bring or encounter.	Managers actively support staff to use coaching conversation techniques (where appropriate) with learners through discussion, team meetings and appraisals.	My institution regularly delivers or provides opportunities for staff to undertake training in coaching or supportive conversational techniques with learners.	Joint practice development opportunities on coaching learners are routinely resourced and encouraged by managers to explore current practice and new ways of working.	There is evidence of a positive correlation between the increase and improvement of coaching conversations and the impact on some key performance indicators.

The self-assessment system is available as a free download from the publisher's website and the authors' websites (all listed at the start of the book).

Taking it further

Jackson, P and McKergow, M (2007) *The Solutions Focus: Making Coaching and Change SIMPLE* (2nd revised edition). London: Nicholas Brealey International.

Thomson, B (2013) *Non-Directive Coaching: Attitudes, Approaches and Applications.* Northwich: Critical Publishing.

Van Nieuwerburgh, C (2012) *Coaching in Education: Getting Better Results for Students, Educators and Parents (Professional Coaching) (The Professional Coaching Series).* London: Karnac Books Ltd.

Whitmore, J (2009) *Coaching for Performance: GROWing Human Potential and Purpose – the Principles and Practice of Coaching and Leadership* (4th edition). London: Nicholas Brealey Publishing.

References

British Broadcasting Corporation (2012) *'Tackle Root Causes' of Pupils' Behaviour.* [online] Available at: www.bbc.co.uk/news/education-19048288 [accessed May 2015].

Hawkins, S and Smith, N (2006) *Coaching, Mentoring and Organisational Consultancy: Supervision and Development.* Maidenhead: McGraw-Hill Education.

Huppert, F A (2006) Positive Emotions and Cognition: Developmental, Neuroscience and Health Perspectives in Forgas, J P (ed.) *Affect in Social Thinking and Behavior,* New York: Psychology Press.

Jackson, P and McKergow, M (2004) cited in Lincoln, S (2004) *Solution-Focused Coaching Training Materials.*

Jackson, P and McKergow, M (2007) *The Solutions Focus: Making Coaching and Change SIMPLE. 2nd revised edition.* London: Nicholas Brealey International.

Lincoln, S (2004) *Solution-Focused Coaching Training Materials.*

Lincoln, S (2012) *Solution-Focused Coaching Skills Toolkit.*

Neenan, M (2009) Using Socratic Questioning in Coaching. *Journal of Rational-Emotive & Cognitive Behavior Therapy,* 27 (4): 249–64.

Palmer, S (2007) PRACTICE: A Model Suitable for Coaching, Counselling, Psychotherapy and Stress Management. *The Coaching Psychologist,* 3 (2): 71–7.

Palmer, S and Szymanska, K (2008) *Cognitive Behavioural Coaching: An Integrative Approach Handbook of Coaching Psychology: A Guide for Practitioners.* New York: Routledge/Taylor and Francis Group.

Whitmore, J (2002) *Coaching for Performance: Growing People, Performance and Purpose* (3rd edition). London: Nicholas Brealey Publishing.

7 Observation

Chapter aims

This chapter helps you to:

- understand how the personal tutor role can be part of an institution's observation scheme and part of the Common Inspection Framework (CIF);

- identify how the personal tutor core values, skills, key activities and procedures relate to specific CIF criteria and are judged by this;

- recognise the benefits of peer observation for the personal tutor role.

Introduction

If the personal tutor role is often given less attention from the institution compared to curriculum teaching, its observation is usually an undeveloped area. This chapter aims to address that.

Critical thinking activity 1

1. List all of the feelings and thoughts that come to mind when you think about observation.

2. Think particularly about being observed in your personal tutor role.

   a. Are there any different feelings or thoughts compared to when you think about a curriculum observation?

   b. Are there any different feelings or thoughts when you think about observation of a group tutorial compared to an observation of a one-to-one with a learner?

3. What about peer observation? Does being observed by one of your trusted colleagues change your thoughts and feelings about observation?

Discussion

1. Your answers are likely to depend very much on how new you are to teaching and personal tutoring. Feelings that may have sprung to mind include nervousness, fear and stress. Thoughts may have included 'extra work on top of everything else'; 'the need to "perform"'; 'will the learners behave, and if not, does that reflect badly on me?' It's important not to beat yourself up about having these feelings and thoughts. Consider the following:

Feeling nervous is a quite natural response to being observed, even for excellent teachers and those with years of experience... any process that feels like a 'test' or presents the risk of failure is always guaranteed to cause some degree of anxiety.

(Wallace, 2013, p 115)

Wallace goes on to say, however, that you can reduce the anxiety by good preparation and rationally approaching your delivery when being observed; for example, by not doing something completely different or out of character (Wallace, 2013, pp 115–6). We agree with this, and using the checklist and other information for group tutorial preparation and delivery from Chapter 4 will hopefully combat any anxiety you may feel and even turn that anxiety into a sense of anticipation.

With that in mind, did any positive feelings or thoughts come to mind; for example, excitement, relishing the challenge and 'the chance to show how well I'm doing things'? This will depend on the preparation process just mentioned and your level of experience, but also on the way staff in your institution perceive observation and the way your institution approaches it. Observation should not be seen as a punitive process but rather a developmental one. As such, you should embrace it, welcome the feedback and use this to the best of your ability for your own development. If you have high expectations of your learners, you need to have high expectations of yourself; and observation gives you an opportunity to judge how you are doing.

These positives are made more likely if your institution has a constructive approach to observation and a 'healthy' culture. For example, it should promote more of an 'open door' approach where being in each other's classrooms is welcomed rather than feared, and move away from the idea of observation as a one-off performance during the year. In addition, these positives can be made more possible by your own individual, positive mindset.

2. You may feel there is less pressure on an observation of your personal tutor role than curriculum teaching since there is usually no qualification attached. However, in our experience of inspection, in Ofsted's eyes there is not a great deal of difference in the way a session will be judged (in a similar way to the minimal differences between good lesson and group tutorial delivery discussed in Chapter 4). Also, likelihood of observation is not necessarily reduced ('if it moves, observe it' was one quote I heard from an Ofsted inspector).

Your confidence in being observed in a group tutorial will be increased by turning back to what we covered in Chapter 4: the tutorial's two main purposes; its similarity to curriculum delivery but slight differences too; the content to be covered and its context in the institution.

The likelihood of being observed applies to one-to-ones with learners too. Here, different skills may be looked at and different feelings will include those of intrusiveness and the somewhat artificial feel of a third party at a one-to-one meeting. Familiarising yourself with the dos and don'ts of one-to-ones with learners in Chapter 4, along with the strengths of Anne's one-to-one with Chloe, both in Chapter 4, should allay some of the fears you may have.

3.   In our experience, peer observation is highly effective for the personal tutor role. The reasons for this are:

- it is supportive and developmental;

- it provides coaching opportunities for you and your peers;

- the giving and receiving of feedback develops the soft skills you are using with learners by enabling you to use them with staff too;

- you are likely to have an established and, hopefully, positive relationship with the other person. Among the key benefits from this is quality of feedback. If there is mutual trust and respect, both sides have permission to offer quite critical feedback because there is the belief that you are 'on the same side' and want to help each other (Wallace, 2013);

- the support of peers is very important when faced with a variety of challenging learner issues;

- the observer (someone in the same role) arguably brings more specific knowledge and understanding;

- it promotes sharing of good practice between people who are doing the same job;

- it can be more low key and low stress. You may feel that you are able to explore and experiment in a non-threatening context;

- it fits in with the 'open door' approach advocated earlier in this discussion.

The format of observation

We have mentioned how your feelings about observation are likely to be affected by how it is approached by your institution and is perceived by the practitioners within it. On the second point, in terms of the FE sector as a whole, according to a recent national project into the use and impact of lesson observation in FE, there is widespread discontent towards it as a form of teacher assessment, with graded models particularly criticised (University and College Union, 2013, p 282).

Although this book is not the place for a detailed discussion of different forms of observation, it is important to note how any negative feelings you have just described may result from the format and approach to observation, along with questioning if it actually helps you to develop, rather than the fact you have to be observed at all. As professionals we are accountable, and observation is part of this accountability; but your resistance or criticism of it could be the result of the *way* you're being held accountable and, if so, according to the recent national project, you are not alone. Based on research findings on the counterproductive consequences of graded observations ('performance-driven models of observation'), Matt O'Leary (2015, p 282) proposes alternative models that are 'development-driven', such as ungraded peer observation and differentiated observation, which get away from 'box-ticking' and appreciate the complexity of the classroom. There have been some recent changes in Ofsted's approach to observation, moving away from graded lesson observations in schools in 2014 and doing the same in FE from September 2015 (Ofsted, 2015a, Inspection Handbook).

The Common Inspection Framework (CIF)

The *Common Inspection Framework (CIF): Education, Skills and Early Years* (Ofsted, 2015b) sets out the principal criteria that inspectors must consider during inspection of every education and training provider. Inspectors will judge your institution on the following four areas:

1. *effectiveness of leadership and management;*

2. *quality of teaching, learning and assessment;*

3. *personal development, behaviour and welfare;*

4. *outcomes for children and other learners.*

(Ofsted, 2015b, CIF)

It is the last three areas that most relate to your personal tutor role.

Critical thinking activity 2

» *Look at Table 7.1. The first column states the judgement criteria for 'quality of teaching, learning and assessment', 'personal development, behaviour and welfare' and 'outcomes for children and other learners'. Complete the other columns showing how the personal tutor core values and skills (Chapter 2) and key activities and procedures (Chapters 4 and 5) relate to, and can influence, these areas. The first one of each has been completed for you. As a reminder, the core values, skills, key activities and procedures are listed for you before the table.*

Core values:

• high expectations;

• approachability;

• diplomacy;

- being non-judgemental;
- compassion;
- the 'equal partner, not superior' approach;
- genuineness.

Core skills:

- building genuine rapport with your learners;
- active listening and questioning;
- challenging;
- reframing;
- reflecting back and summarising;
- teamwork;
- decision-making and problem-solving;
- role modelling;
- proactivity, creativity and innovation;
- working under pressure.

Key activities/procedures:

- the tracking and monitoring of learners;
- one-to-ones with learners;
- group tutorial planning and teaching;
- disciplinary – a positive approach;
- right course review;
- internal progression;
- external progression;
- working with learners who have additional support needs;
- safeguarding.

Table 7.1 *Common Inspection Framework criteria linked with relevant personal tutor core values, skills, key activities and procedures*

CIF criteria	Relevant personal tutor core values and skills (Chapter 2) and key activities and procedures (Chapters 4 and 5) and how they can relate to CIF criteria		
	Core values	Core skills	Key activities/procedures
Quality of teaching, learning and assessment Inspectors will make a judgement on the effectiveness of teaching, learning and assessment by evaluating the extent to which:			
1. Teachers, practitioners and other staff have consistently high expectations of what each child or learner can achieve, including the most able and the most disadvantaged.	High expectations.	Active listening and questioning; challenging; reframing; role modelling.	Tracking and monitoring ensures progress. One-to-ones which monitor progress through effective conversations and target setting. Additional support – any needs are fully supported. Safeguarding.
2. Teachers, practitioners and other staff have a secure understanding of the age group they are working with and have relevant subject knowledge that is detailed and communicated well to children and learners.			
3. Assessment information is gathered from looking at what children and learners already know, understand and can do, and is informed by their parents/previous providers as appropriate.			
4. Assessment information is used to plan appropriate teaching and learning strategies, including to identify children and learners who are falling behind in their learning or who need additional support, enabling children and learners to make good progress and achieve well.			

Table 7.1 (cont.)

CIF criteria	Relevant personal tutor core values and skills (Chapter 2) and key activities and procedures (Chapters 4 and 5) and how they can relate to CIF criteria		
	Core values	Core skills	Key activities/procedures
5. Except in the case of the very young, children and learners understand how to improve as a result of useful feedback from staff and, where relevant, parents, carers and employers understand how learners should improve and how they can contribute to this.			
6. Engagement with parents, carers and employers helps them to understand how children and learners are doing in relation to the standards expected and what they need to do to improve.			
7. Equality of opportunity and recognition of diversity are promoted through teaching and learning.			
8. Where relevant, English, mathematics and other skills necessary to function as an economically active member of British society and globally are promoted through teaching and learning.			
Personal development, behaviour and welfare Inspectors will make a judgement on the personal development, behaviour and welfare of children and learners by evaluating the extent to which the provision is successfully promoting and supporting children's and other learners':			

	High expectations; 'equal partner not superior' approach; genuineness.	Challenging; role modelling; proactivity, creativity and innovation.	Tracking and monitoring ensures learners maintain commitment to their studies. Praise and encouragement in one-to-ones helps learners take pride in their work. If appropriate, positive learning conversations to fully engage and motivate learners.			
9. Pride in achievement and commitment to learning, supported by a positive culture across the whole provider.						
10. Self-confidence, self-awareness and understanding of how to be a successful learner.						
11. Choices about the next stage of their education, employment, self-employment or training, where relevant, from impartial careers advice and guidance.						
12. Where relevant, employability skills so that they are well prepared for the next stage of their education, employment, self-employment or training.						
13. Prompt and regular attendance.						
14. Following of any guidelines for behaviour and conduct, including management of their own feelings and behaviour, and how they relate to others.						
15. Understanding of how to keep themselves safe from relevant risks such as abuse, sexual exploitation and extremism, including when using the internet and social media.						

Table 7.1 (cont.)

CIF criteria	Relevant personal tutor core values and skills (Chapter 2) and key activities and procedures (Chapters 4 and 5) and how they can relate to CIF criteria		
	Core values	Core skills	Key activities/procedures
16. Knowledge of how to keep themselves healthy, both emotionally and physically, including through exercising and healthy eating.			
17. Personal development, so that they are well prepared to respect others and contribute to wider society and life in Britain.			
Outcomes for children and other learners Inspectors will take account of current standards and progress, including the provider's own data, and make a relevant judgement on academic and other learning outcomes for children and learners by evaluating the extent to which they:			
18. Progress well from their different starting points and achieve or exceed standards expected for their age.	High expectations.	Active listening and questioning; challenging; reframing; problem-solving.	Tracking and monitoring learners' progress; one-to-ones with effective target setting; additional support and safeguarding – any relevant issues affecting progress are addressed.
19. Attain relevant qualifications so that they can and do progress to the next stage of their education into courses that lead to higher-level qualifications and into jobs that meet local and national needs.			

(Ofsted, 2015a, pp 13–14)

Critical thinking activity 3

» *Have a look at the extracts from three different observer feedback reports given for one-to-ones and a further three for group tutorials in the Table 7.2. Complete the table by identifying which section of the CIF each relates to (using the numbers from Table 7.1) and, by interpreting the language used in the extracts, decide whether it is a strength or an area for development. Again, the first of each has been completed for you.*

Table 7.2 Extracts from observer feedback reports linked to the CIF

Extracts from one-to-one observation feedback reports	Which section of the CIF it relates to	Strength or area for development?
You engaged the learner well using open questioning. Particularly effective was how you clarified his step-by-step progress and gave him a sense of purpose by agreeing challenging targets. Also, you drew out what he found most enjoyable about the course and linked this to his long-term career aim.	1; 5; 10; 11; 18	Strength
The learner said she wasn't enjoying a part of the course but you moved past this quickly onto more positive things. You did the majority of the talking in the one-to-one meeting and finished off her sentences on a few occasions.		
This was a challenging one-to-one to carry out since the learner was not confident in speaking out. However, you handled it sensitively showing you cared ('how can I help with that?'). You displayed compassion by bringing in your own personal experience of nerves and how you overcame them while still reinforcing that everyone is different. He responded positively, well done.		
Extracts from group tutorial observation feedback reports	**Which section of the CIF it relates to**	**Strength or area for development?**
You got the learners to think about what reflection is, good. However, then they were asked to do this and some struggled. They could have been given some examples of good reflection compared to poor reflection and this could have been linked to employability skills.	10; 12; 14	Area for development

Table 7.2 (cont.)

Extracts from group tutorial observation feedback reports	Which section of the CIF it relates to	Strength or area for development?
You effectively tailored the session (on time management) to the learners' vocational area. In addition, prior to this, the small group activity really got the learners to engage and make individualised responses. Those more confident were stretched by the extension tasks you gave them.		
This was a session on a sensitive subject (drugs and alcohol). Some learners made controversial and inappropriate comments. This was rather 'glossed over'. If ground rules or boundaries have been set for the group it would have been helpful to revisit these at the beginning of the session (for example 'respect each other's views'). Clustering tables into small groups and dividing the whole group can also help group dynamics and prevent louder learners from dominating.		

Both critical thinking activities have highlighted just how relevant the personal tutor core values, skills, key activities and procedures are to what inspectors view as important. You should note that the CIF is liable to change over time, so ensure you keep abreast of any changes.

All institutional internal observation schemes will differ slightly. For example, they may be graded or non-graded. However, all are likely to reflect the Ofsted judgement criteria already discussed. Where group tutorial and one-to-one observation fits into this is also likely to differ.

Summary

Observation can easily be seen as another layer of stress that you could do without in your busy working life. However, if you are embodying the personal tutor core values and carrying out the associated core skills, key activities and working within the key procedures effectively, with the help of this chapter you can clearly see how much of the Common Inspection Framework criteria are met. Moreover, on the road to outstanding personal tutoring you should use observation as a developmental tool and, as such, welcome rather than fear it.

Undertaking effective peer observation is a key enabler in achieving this. Previously we have talked much about the use of soft skills with learners. Giving and receiving feedback within such a process also develops these skills with fellow staff members.

Learning checklist

Tick off each point when you feel confident you understand it.

☐ *I can see how observation can be beneficial to my personal tutor practice and how it can be a positive experience.*

☐ *I understand the benefit of peer observation for the personal tutor role.*

☐ *I understand how the personal tutor core values, skills, key activities and procedures relate to specific CIF criteria.*

☐ *I can identify how real-world examples of one-to-one and group tutorial practice relate to CIF criteria and can judge whether they are strengths or areas for development.*

Critical reflections

1. To what extent do you think that observation is viewed as punitive or developmental by staff in your institution? Does anything need to be done to change the attitude towards observation, and if so, what?

2. Is peer observation used in your institution? If not, how could it be implemented? If it is, are there improvements that could be made?

3. Discuss how your teacher training course, teaching placement or current institution prepares you for observations of one-to-ones with learners and group tutorials.

4. To what extent do you think outcomes from observation of your group tutorials and one-to-ones effectively develop your practice in these? What do you think could be done to further improve this?

5. To what extent does your institution relate your personal tutor role to the CIF criteria? What could be done to further improve this?

Personal tutor self-assessment system

See following table.

PERSONAL TUTOR SELF-ASSESSMENT SYSTEM: Chapter 7 observation

	Minimum standard 2 points	Bronze 4 points	Silver 6 points	Gold 8 points	Platinum 10 points
Individual	I am aware how personal tutor practice can be improved through observation and reflection on observation feedback and outcomes.	I discuss the personal tutor core skills with colleagues and my line manager as a result of observation, both informally and in appraisal. I undertake peer observation.	I am developing my soft skills through giving and receiving feedback in peer observation. I reflect and develop my personal tutor practice through this process and enable others to do the same. I can link specific CIF criteria to personal tutor practice.	I am seeing improvements from the work I am doing on specific improvement targets (related to personal tutor practice) resulting from observation. I review these regularly myself and with my line manager.	I use outcomes from peer observation, the institution's observation scheme and inspection to rigorously improve my personal tutor practice. I jointly develop practice with colleagues on a regular basis.
Institutional	My institution's observation scheme includes observation of group tutorials and one-to-ones, and relevant staff are communicated with about what the approach and criteria are.	Outcomes from observations include comments on personal tutor core skills and inform line managers' discussions and appraisal with delivery staff. Informal and peer observations are routinely practised.	Specific personal tutor core skills are included in improvement targets and observation feedback. These are reviewed regularly by line managers with their staff. Personal tutors can link specific CIF criteria to personal tutor practice.	My institution's observation scheme and approach through informal observations are viewed both as developmental and supportive. A culture of joint practice development in personal tutor core skills results.	There is an important emphasis on personal tutor core skills in the institution's informal and formal observation schemes. These skills and inspection feedback on them are comprehensively included in outcomes which form part of a cycle of continuous quality improvement.

The self-assessment system is available as a free download from the publisher's website and the authors' websites (all listed at the start of the book).

Taking it further

Kirkman, L and Wallace, I (2014) *Pimp Your Lesson: Prepare, Innovate, Motivate and Perfect* (3rd edition). London: Bloomsbury.

Ofsted (2015) *Better Inspection for All: A Report on the Responses to the Consultation*. Manchester: Ofsted. Available at: www.gov.uk/government/uploads/system/uploads/attachment_data/file/400625/Better_inspection_for_all_consultation_response_FINAL_2_.pdf [accessed May 2015].

O'Leary, M (2013) Surveillance, Performativity and Normalised Practice: The Use and Impact of Graded Lesson Observations in Further Education Colleges. *Journal of Further and Higher Education*, 37 (5): 694–714.

O'Leary, M (2014) *Classroom Observation: A Guide to the Effective Observation of Teaching and Learning*. London: Routledge.

References

Gravells, J and Wallace, S (2013) *The A-Z Guide to Working in Further Education*. Northwich: Critical Publishing.

O'Leary, M (2015) Measurement as an Obstacle to Improvement: Moving Beyond the Limitations of Graded Lesson Observations in Gregson M, Nixon L, Pollard A and Hillier Y (eds) *Readings for Reflective Teaching in Further, Adult and Vocational Education*. London: Bloomsbury.

Ofsted (2015a) *The Common Inspection Framework: Education, Skills and Early Years*. Ofsted: Manchester. Available at: www.gov.uk/government/publications/common-inspection-framework-education-skills-and-early-years-from-september-2015 [accessed June 2015].

Ofsted (2015b) *Further Education and Skills Inspection Handbook*. Ofsted: Manchester. Available at: www.gov.uk/government/publications/further-education-and-skills-inspection-handbook-from-september-2015 [accessed June 2015].

University and College Union (2013), *Developing a National Framework for the Effective Use of Lesson Observation in Further Education*. Project Report for the University and College Union. Available at: www.ucu.org.uk/media/pdf/i/q/ucu_lessonobsproject_nov13.pdf [accessed August 2015].

8 Reflective practice

Chapter aims

This chapter helps you to:

- identify the difference between reflection and reflective practice;

- understand why reflective practice is important for your role as a personal tutor;

- consider the benefits of, and potential barriers to, effective reflective practice for your personal tutor role as well as for the institution you work for;

- explore a number of reflective practice models and apply these to typical personal tutoring scenarios.

Critical thinking activity 1

» *In preparation for this chapter, it is important to consider what you already understand about reflection and reflective practice and how this contributes to your beliefs and attitudes as a personal tutor. Copy and complete Figure 8.1, filling in the empty boxes by stating your current thoughts on reflective practice. You could include benefits, barriers to carrying it out, relevance or importance to your personal tutor role. Try to make your statements as specific as possible because this will provide you with a reference point and help you in understanding and implementing reflective practice in the future.*

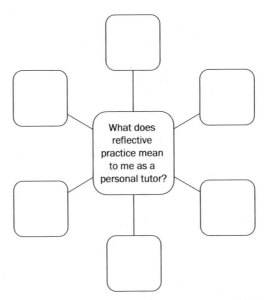

Figure 8.1 *What does reflective practice mean to me as a personal tutor?*

What do we mean by reflection and reflective practice?

Reflection and reflective practice are important tools to enable professionals to learn from their own experiences. Although they are very similar and complement each other as part of a continuous learning cycle, there are subtle differences between them.

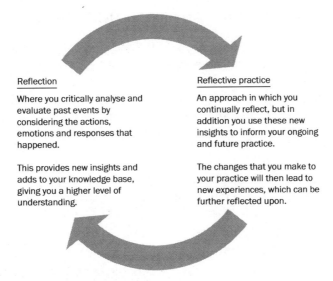

Reflection

Where you critically analyse and evaluate past events by considering the actions, emotions and responses that happened.

This provides new insights and adds to your knowledge base, giving you a higher level of understanding.

Reflective practice

An approach in which you continually reflect, but in addition you use these new insights to inform your ongoing and future practice.

The changes that you make to your practice will then lead to new experiences, which can be further reflected upon.

Figure 8.2 *Reflection and reflective practice*

As mentioned at the start of the book, whether you are a trainee or an experienced practitioner, finding time in the 'whirlwind' of teaching and personal tutoring can be a challenge due to the numerous demands placed on you by your learners and the institution you work for. When you've found a minute, how often have you stopped what you're doing for a *useful* and *significant* period of time and thought about your experiences in an organised way to make sense of them? Valuable thinking or reflection opportunities (and hopefully you've had time for some) provide you with the chance to contemplate the aspects of your practice which you would like to change or develop; for example, whether something could work better the next time you try it. Hopefully this valuable reflection time is happening routinely, either on your own or with your mentor; but if not, in order to continually professionally develop, it should be incorporated into your routine at some point within your working week.

Improving your classroom teaching through reflective practice is widely considered as vital for both trainees and experienced practitioners to continually improve, and it is no different when it comes to your personal tutoring role. Fundamentally, reflection involves thinking deeply about an experience in order for you to understand it and hopefully make sense of it. However, reflection alone is not sufficient to stimulate effective learning and improve your personal tutor practice. Even if you regularly reflect on your practice, ten years' experience as a personal tutor may consist of ten years doing the same thing in the same way. The key principle is to regularly act on your reflections, informed by your practice and the opinions of others, which will ensure that effective learning and continuous professional development happens and that your reflections develop into reflective practice.

Throughout your teacher training course and teaching career you are likely to encounter a significant number of theorists, definitions and models related to this topic, some of which are explored in the section of this chapter on models of reflective practice and are also listed in Taking it further. What this chapter does is to contextualise reflective practice for your personal tutor role.

Reflective practice for your personal tutor role

Why is reflective practice important for you as a personal tutor? The answer is, simply because a large proportion of your time as a personal tutor involves supporting learners individually and this requires a great deal of focus, emotional energy, adaptability, decision-making and, most of all, skill. The learned ability to carry out the activities and display the skills of a personal tutor in an outstanding way cannot just be honed through reading a book or just doing it. Time must be taken to reflect on your experiences, to learn from them and become better.

In terms of your personal tutor role, the following key points highlight what reflective practice is and isn't, as well as the expected benefits and challenges of undertaking this activity regularly.

It is:

✓   a time to think clearly, be honest and consider the facts of your chosen episode for reflection;

✓   an activity which can be undertaken individually or with another person (for example a mentor or trusted colleague);

✓   a process which should be undertaken regularly, for example once a week;

✓   a skill which can be learnt and honed;

✓   an activity which should be undertaken alongside other professional development activities, such as peer observation, training and work shadowing;

✓   about applying critical analysis to your reflection, such as:

    ○   what actually happened (good and bad)

    ○   what everyone's feelings were at the time

    ○   what else you could have done or done differently

    ○   what you might choose to do differently next time.

It is not:

✗   something you need less as your experience as a personal tutor increases;

✗   a waste of your planning and development time;

✗   an easy thing to do, because critically analysing yourself can mean asking tough, probing questions.

The benefits of reflection are as follows.

•   It improves your ability to view events clearly and more objectively.

•   It helps you to respond more positively to difficult issues or problems.

•   If carried out with a trusted colleague or mentor, it enables you to 'offload' any difficult or emotional issues in a structured, positive and supportive way (sometimes referred to as 'supervision' within other fields).

•   It reduces stress and feelings of anxiety.

•   It reduces feelings of isolation and combats a culture of individualism, particularly when undertaken with a trusted colleague.

•   It helps you to identify your personal strengths and relative limitations and to gain new professional insights.

•   It improves your confidence, professional judgement and practice as a personal tutor.

•   It creates a positive, continuous professional development cycle when undertaken regularly.

•   It provides better provision of teaching, personal tutoring and coaching.

The challenges of reflection are as follows.

•   It can be difficult to find the time to do properly.

- You may lack the experience and/or knowledge to make sense of some issues. This could lead to you following the models more 'mechanically' and not reflecting critically or deeply enough to fully understand the real issue(s). Undertaking reflection with your mentor or an experienced, trusted colleague would help to mitigate this.

- As it requires a critical and honest approach, you could find that you view your areas for improvement as failures, instead of an opportunity to learn and develop. Therefore resilience and a positive attitude is needed.

- You may fear that if you discuss your moments of reflection (such as examples of poor judgement) openly with colleagues, you may be jeopardising or damaging your reputation.

- The educational institution's culture and processes may not actively support you and other personal tutors to be honest and open in your moments of reflection.

Models of reflective practice

Models, sometimes known as frameworks, of reflective practice encourage a structured process to guide your thinking, learning and your application of new knowledge. There are a number of models and theories that you can choose from; however, it is important to recognise there is no 'correct' model. Ensure you choose the one that feels most comfortable to assist you in learning from your personal tutoring experiences. In this section we will consider a range of models from David Kolb, Graham Gibbs, Chris Johns and Stephen Brookfield. However, there are more models and theories of reflective practice to research and use, such as Atkins and Murphy (1994), Dewey (1933), Schön (1983) and Rolfe *et al*. (2001), to name but a few. Our experience has shown that it can be useful and appropriate to use one model of reflective practice as a basis, but use prompt questions from other models if they best fit your particular situation. Therefore, our advice is to try a number of models and, through trial and error, find which best suits your needs as a personal tutor and even, possibly, create your own personal reflective practice model.

The Experiential Learning Cycle: David Kolb

David Kolb's publications, notably his book *Experiential Learning: Experience as The Source Of Learning and Development* (1984) and the development of his Experiential Learning Cycle theory, have been acknowledged as seminal in developing our understanding of human learning behaviour. In essence, the cycle means 'learning from experience' and is typically represented by a four-stage cycle. Kolb viewed learning as an integrated process, with each stage being mutually supportive of, and feeding into, the next. It is possible to enter the cycle at any point and follow through the sequence; however, Kolb believed that 'effective learning' only occurs when you are able to execute all four stages of the model, therefore suggesting that no one stage of the cycle is an effective learning process in isolation.

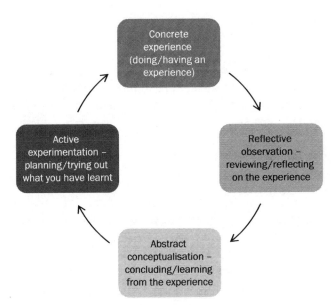

Figure 8.3 Kolb's Experiential Learning Cycle (1984) – adapted

Concrete experience

The concrete experience is the 'doing' element, which stems from your actual experience of personal tutor practice.

Reflective observation

The reflective observation component of the model derives from your analysis and judgements of events relating to delivery and support activities that you engage in as a personal tutor. You are likely to naturally reflect on your experiences, particularly if you are new to the personal tutor role and possibly less confident in your knowledge and ability. It is very common for practitioners who are new to the personal tutor role to work with a learner on a one-to-one basis or in a group tutorial and come out of that experience and think that it went well or badly in an intuitive sense. This 'common sense reflection' (a phrase coined by Jennifer Moon, 2004, p 82) is a useful starting point, but how do you really know what was good and bad, and why?

Essentially, you need to articulate these thoughts or reflections in a clear and systematic way so that you can remember what you thought in order to build on that experience. Examples of ways to capture and crystallise your thoughts could be through keeping a journal of your reflections after one-to-ones and group tutorials or after any significant event at work (see Brookfield's suggestions for reflective journals later in this section). Other useful information which will feed into and add to this holistic reflection might be formal observations of your practice by your mentor, peer observation, appraisals and learner feedback.

Abstract conceptualisation

So that you can plan what you might do differently in the future, in addition to your reflections on your experience you also need to be informed by wider reading and educational theory. This may be through reading a book such as this one, researching on the internet or in journals, attending a training session or speaking to someone who you feel may have sufficient experience in that area. In essence, this section allows you to bring together the theory and analysis from the reflective observation stage, which will allow you to form conclusions about your personal tutoring practice.

Active experimentation

The conclusions you formed from the abstract conceptualisation stage will now form the basis by which you can plan the changes to your practice and turn your reflections into reflective practice. This is where the cycle starts again; in other words, active experimentation is where you put into action the desired changes you want in your role as a personal tutor in order to create another concrete experience and thereby create a continuous professional development cycle.

The Reflective Cycle: Graham Gibbs

Graham Gibbs' (1998) Reflective Cycle model provides useful prompt questions to guide your reflections. It encourages a clear description of the situation, analysis and evaluation

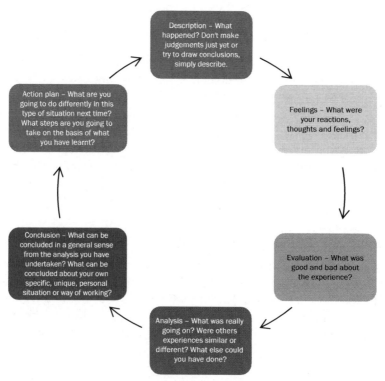

Figure 8.4 *Gibbs' Reflective Cycle (1998) – adapted*

of feelings, the event, your experience, as well as examining how you might change your practice in the future. As a personal tutor, you will work with learners on a one-to-one basis regularly, and an effective way of capturing learning from ad hoc experiences during these one-to-ones is to review completed reflections together as a set to identify any patterns or trends in your practice which may not be immediately obvious from just looking at one reflection. If you choose this model for your reflections, in theory you should follow the six stages, with each one informing the next. The analysis section is where you will need to use discursive, analytical writing. The other sections require mainly statements of description, statements of value (whether something was good or bad) and statements of summation or statements of justification (why something was done).

Model of Structured Reflection: Chris Johns

Chris Johns' (1995) model, similar to Gibbs' model, provides useful prompt questions to stimulate and structure your thoughts. His model can be used individually; however, he supports the idea of undertaking reflective practice with an experienced colleague and refers to this as 'guided reflection'. Talking to your colleagues about what happens when you work with learners can sometimes, sadly, become a rare experience after you become qualified. Even though, for the majority of people, reflective practice itself is an intensely personal process, valuable discussions with another can help shed new light on your experiences as a personal tutor, and even though you may not find a solution, it can be reassuring and sometimes motivating to realise that what you thought were your own idiosyncratic failings are in fact experiences that are shared by others who work in similar settings.

Outstanding personal tutors develop a high level of rapport with learners while maintaining a clear professional boundary, and as a result they tend to find out a lot more about their learners than some of their fellow colleagues. Furthermore, it is likely that you will find out a lot more about your learners through your personal tutoring role, because of working with them in one-to-ones, than through your teaching role. The things that you find out can really affect your emotions; these can range from feeling happy and proud through to being upset, anxious and distressed. This is why we believe that peer reflective practice is a very useful tool for your personal tutoring role. Another person's point of view takes away some of the subjectivity from the reflection, which can be more effective in making sense of, and dealing with, difficult issues.

Even though Johns' model isn't portrayed as cyclical, it is advisable to treat it as such and begin each reflective practice session at the description phase. His questions have not been designed to be asked in a particular order, although there is a progression within the questions. Also, you don't have to use all of the questions in every reflective practice session, and, if appropriate, you can use any question more than once.

Johns' Model of Structured Reflection (1995): adapted

Stage 1: Description

- Write a description of the experience.

- What are the key issues within this description that I need to pay attention to?

Stage 2: Reflection

- What was I trying to achieve?
- Why did I act as I did?
- What are the consequences of my actions for the following:
  - the learners;
  - myself;
  - the people I work with?
- How did I feel about this experience when it was happening?
- How did the learner/colleague feel about it?
- How do I know how the learner/colleague felt about it?

Stage 3: Influencing factors

- What internal factors influenced my decision-making and actions?
- What external factors influenced my decision-making and actions?
- What sources of knowledge did influence or should have influenced my decision-making and actions?

Stage 4: Alternative strategies

- Could I have dealt with the situation better?
- What other choices did I have?
- What would be the consequences of these other choices?

Stage 5: Learning

- How can I make sense of this experience in light of past experience and future practice?
- How do I feel about this experience now?
- Have I taken effective action to support myself and others as a result of this experience?

Four Critically Reflective Lenses: Stephen Brookfield

Even though Stephen Brookfield relates his thinking on reflective practice to the traditional teaching role, we feel some of his suggestions are equally relevant to the personal tutor role, and in places we have adapted them to fit this.

In order to succeed in becoming critically reflective, Brookfield (1995, pp 29–30) asserts that teachers must view themselves through four critically reflective lenses, which are:

1. Our autobiographies as learners and teachers: using our own unique personal self-reflection and collecting the insights and meanings for teaching.

2. Our students' eyes: making an assessment of one's self through the learners' lens by seeking their input and seeing classrooms and learning from their perspectives.

3. Our colleagues' experiences: by peer review of teaching from colleagues' experiences, observations and feedback.

4. Theoretical literature: by frequently referring to the theoretical literature that may provide an alternative, interpretive framework for a situation.

Teachers are required to undertake some of the four aspects of Brookfield's model as part of their teacher training course and other aspects are likely to be built into the processes of the institution that you work within. A key aspect, which you may not have been asked to carry out as a personal tutor, is keeping a reflective journal – in Brookfield's terms a 'Teaching Log' (stage one of his model), in our terms a 'personal tutor log'.

Brookfield (1995) argues that it is useful for teachers to keep a weekly record of the events that have impressed themselves most vividly on their consciousness, particularly focusing on events that caused them particular pleasure, stress or puzzlement. He argues that one of the principal benefits for teachers of becoming critically reflective is to ground them emotionally, and this is certainly useful within the personal tutor role due to the multitude of issues you can be faced with. In order to make this personal tutor log a feasible task, try filling in the journal weekly for 15 to 20 minutes. Brookfield (1995) recommends some of the following questions and suggests that you should jot down any brief responses that seem appropriate.

- What was (were) the moment(s) this week when I felt most connected, engaged or affirmed as a personal tutor – the moment(s) I said to myself, 'This is what being a personal tutor is really about'?

- What was (were) the moment(s) this week when I felt most disconnected, disengaged or bored as a personal tutor – the moment(s) I said to myself, 'I'm just going through the motions here'?

- What was the situation that caused me the greatest anxiety or distress – the kind of situation that I kept replaying in my mind as I was dropping off to sleep, or that caused me to say to myself, 'I don't want to go through this again for a while'?

- What was the event that most took me by surprise – an event where I saw or did something that shook me up, caught me off guard, knocked me off my stride, gave me a jolt, or made me unexpectedly happy?

- Of everything I did this week in my personal tutor role, what would I do differently if I had the chance to do it again?

- What do I feel proudest of in my personal tutoring activities this week and why?

Despite the fact that our personal tutoring experiences run the risk of being dismissed as '*merely anecdotal*', Brookfield, while conceding that '*all experience is inherently idiosyncratic*', asserts that our autobiographies are '*one of the most important sources of insight into teaching to which we have access*' (1995, p 31). Regularly updating a personal tutor log is a good way to begin to make reflective practice more of a routine and less of a one-off when the need arises, and it will produce benefits for your ongoing professional development as a personal tutor.

Critical thinking activity 2

From your experience of working with learners so far, think of one personal tutoring scenario which you feel didn't go to plan and wished the outcome could have been better (for you or the learner). Using your preferred reflective practice model, answer the following questions.

1. Are there multiple issues for reflection from this single scenario? If so, list them.

2. What is the key issue for critical reflection?

3. Focusing on the key issue, note down your thoughts for each stage of your reflective practice model and how you could use this new knowledge to make improvements in your practice.

Scenarios for you to reflect on

All moments of reflection are different and have varying levels of complexity. Therefore, they require differing levels of analysis and evaluation and also require you to focus on different aspects of your reflective practice model. On occasion, trainee teachers and personal tutors may feel that some aspects require more urgent consideration than experienced practitioners do. Teachers new to the reflective process are often tempted to engage with the action plan part of their model more quickly and readily than the other preceding stages. This should be avoided to ensure there is greater consistency between your analysis and course of action. Irrespective of your starting point, you need to engage in the process, recognising that you need to be open, honest and authentic throughout to really benefit; realising that critical reflection will on occasion create uncomfortable professional awareness but ultimately will lead you towards becoming an outstanding personal tutor.

The following scenario illustrates a potential situation that you could encounter within your personal tutor role. After the explanation of the scenario there is a list of points that contain some further questions and thoughts which could inform the stages of your reflective practice.

Scenario 1: group tutorial

During a group tutorial on the topic of sexuality with a lively class, a small group of learners make inappropriate comments regarding sexuality to two other learners which you overhear. You firmly address the individuals in question, but the comments between the two groups become more heated and offensive as the class continues. Eventually, arguments break out between different groups. You regain order, but the session is about to finish and the arguments appear to continue in the corridor.

Group tutorial potential reflection considerations

- From my knowledge of the group and in the planning stages for this session, were there any potential issues that I could have pre-empted and taken action to overcome? For example, could I have used a different seating plan?

- Did I establish clear boundaries before starting the session either at the start of the academic year or within the previous group tutorial?

- Did I reiterate or even need to reiterate the consequences for any poor behaviour within the classroom?

- Were the learning activities and content suitable for this age group and level of learners?

- Was the approach to discipline fair and appropriate in light of the comments made? Did the approach to discipline follow the institution's guidelines and procedures?

- Should I have kept some or all of the learners involved behind afterwards to address the situation?

- What are other colleagues' feelings about these learners and this incident?

- Has this type of issue or any other issue happened before between these groups of learners?

- How old are the learners and do their parents/guardians need to be made aware of what has happened?

Critical thinking activity 3

Having read the example personal tutoring scenario, consider the following two scenarios within your current educational institution and with your learners. Then, imagining that you are the personal tutor in each scenario, answer the following questions.

1. Are there multiple issues for reflection? If so, list all of the potential issues in a similar way to the worked example (see the considerations from the previous scenario).

2. What is the key issue for critical reflection?

Possible reflection considerations are provided in the discussion section that follows the scenarios. However, try to complete the activity before reading these.

Scenario 2

You are supporting Helen, a very academically capable learner, through one-to-one meetings. She wants to achieve high grades in her A levels so that she can study medicine at the university that she chooses. However, after a recent poor exam result her motivation and confidence drops dramatically and she begins to miss many of the SMART targets you had co-created. She regularly comes to see you for advice as her personal tutor and, even though you have many other things to do, you try to find time to help her.

Scenario 3

One of your learners, Scott, has been displaying poor behaviour in class and is falling behind with handing in his coursework. On numerous occasions you have tried to have positive learning conversations with him, but he refuses to talk about these issues, which you find frustrating and, even though you don't want to, you can't help showing it. You eventually get him to talk about the issues, but he just blames everyone else, such as his teachers and fellow learners.

Discussion

Scenario 2: reflection considerations

*   Were the initial SMART targets too ambitious or about right?

*   It is important to remember that Helen's academic ability won't have faltered significantly in such a short space of time and to make her aware of this.

*   Other than the recent poor exam result, were there any other factors that have contributed to the dip in her performance?

*   Due to the short space of time that Helen needs to turn things around, what are some small key things that you can discuss with her so that she has the best chance of achieving her aim? If it is more of a confidence/motivation issue, what are some small steps she can take to regain this? When a learner is facing a confidence/ motivation issue, finding ways to achieve 'quick wins' is a useful way to create momentum towards a goal and make it feel more achievable.

*   What do her other teachers say about her past and current performance? When you have identified a way forward with Helen, it would be sensible to reassess the previous SMART targets to see if they are still suitable.

Scenario 3: reflection considerations

*   How long has Scott been displaying poor behaviour? Is it a recent issue or more of a long-term pattern?

*   What are the *immediate, visible* reasons for Scott's poor behaviour and drop in performance? (For example, tired from working too much or staying up or being out too late, issues with fellow learners or friends.)

*   What do Scott's other teachers say about his behaviour and performance in class?

*   Are there any additional support needs which Scott may have? Is the institution providing/can the institue provide support for this?

- Are there any underlying root causes behind this behaviour? (In other words, not immediately visible; for example a mental health problem, an unidentified learning difficulty or issues at home.)

- You are human and we can't help feeling frustrated and even showing it from time to time at work. That said, if possible, try to not show this frustration to Scott unless you feel it will have the desired effect of helping him to improve.

- Poor behaviour which affects the learning of others isn't acceptable. The educational institution should provide support and procedures for you and your colleagues to address this.

- It is unlikely that you will see an immediate improvement until Scott firstly recognises the behavioural issue and takes ownership of his actions, which should be one of your primary goals.

- In order to really support Scott and address this issue you need to explore issues above and below the surface to help him effect real change. Of course, an obvious constraint when trying to do this is time. Start with the immediate and visible reasons to see if this has the desired effect before moving onto other potential reasons or issues, which may take more time and be harder to identify.

Summary

We have said before that personal tutoring can sometimes take a back seat in comparison with curriculum delivery. If this is the case, it could well be that your reflections, until now, have mainly been concerned with curriculum delivery rather than personal tutoring. However, the road to becoming an outstanding personal tutor will consist of many challenging situations and emotive issues, thus making reflection and reflective practice in relation to your personal tutoring activities highly important.

Reflective practice is more than just thinking about what happened; it is an approach of continually reflecting through using a systematic process of collecting, recording and analysing thoughts and observations from yourself as well as trusted colleagues. It enables you to use development time effectively to focus on, or discuss, what has actually happened and consider why. It isn't an easy or quick thing to do. However, by undertaking the process regularly, you will be able to transfer learning from one situation to similar future events and, therefore, you will be less likely to jump to conclusions about situations and you will develop more constructive ideas regarding your personal tutor practice.

To aid your development, we recommend keeping a personal tutor log at the end of each week or after an incident that feels particularly significant with a learner (or even a colleague). Furthermore, consider discussing your reflections and potential actions with a trusted colleague or even read up about a particular subject and, as a result, you may try to do something differently or possibly decide that what you were doing was the best way.

Learning checklist

Tick off each point when you feel confident you understand it.

☐ *I understand that reflective practice is an approach through which I should regularly reflect on my practice as a personal tutor and use the resulting insights to inform my ongoing actions and future practice.*

☐ *I understand that reflection and reflective practice can be undertaken either individually or with a trusted colleague, mentor or friend.*

☐ *I know that the choice over which model of reflective practice I use isn't as important as the emphasis I place on being honest in the process as well as identifying what aspects of my personal tutor practice I would change if the incident or issue arose again.*

☐ *I recognise that being critically reflective of my personal tutoring practice is likely to highlight areas for development. I know that I shouldn't view these as my 'failures' but as my opportunities to learn and improve.*

☐ *I appreciate that it is useful to review completed reflections together as a set to identify patterns or trends in my practice which may not be immediately obvious from looking at just one reflection.*

☐ *I understand that keeping a personal tutor log is a good way to ensure that I make reflective practice part of my professional development routine.*

Critical reflections

1. From your experience of working as a personal tutor so far:

   a. identify two potential barriers to making reflective practice an ongoing, regular activity;

   b. for each potential barrier, explain one small action you could take to overcome it.

2. Which would you find more effective and why: undertaking reflective practice individually or in dialogue with a trusted person?

3. Identify the key opportunity costs of personal tutors not undertaking reflective practice for the:

   a. individual;

   b. educational institution.

4. Evaluate whether reflective practice is equally important for an experienced practitioner and a newly qualified practitioner.

Personal tutor self-assessment system

See following table.

PERSONAL TUTOR SELF-ASSESSMENT SYSTEM: *Chapter 8 reflective practice*

	Minimum standard 2 points	Bronze 4 points	Silver 6 points	Gold 8 points	Platinum 10 points
Individual	I regularly think about what is working well and what could be improved within my personal tutoring practice.	I carry out reflective practice, related to my personal tutor role, as an ongoing, regular activity.	In response to what I am learning from the reflective practice process, I am seeing incremental improvements in my personal tutoring practice.	In response to what I am learning from the reflective practice process, I am seeing incremental improvements in my learners' experience and their educational outcomes.	The outcomes of my reflective practice inform joint practice development projects with colleagues.
Institutional	My institution values the professional development of its personal tutors and actively encourages this through providing opportunities to discuss practice and attend training events.	My institution displays its commitment to its personal tutors undertaking effective individual or peer reflective practice through providing adequate time, resources and support for the process. Honest and open dialogue about critical incidents or issues is embraced as positive and developmental.	Line managers value the benefits reflective practice can bring to personal tutors and they actively encourage its use within meetings, individual discussions and appraisals.	Peer and individual reflective practice is routinely used by all personal tutors within the institution.	Action research projects and joint practice development opportunities are routinely used by personal tutors as two of the ways to further develop and disseminate the learning from the reflective practice process.

The self-assessment system is available as a free download from the publisher's website and the authors' websites (all listed at the start of the book).

Taking it further

Appleyard, K and Appleyard, N (2015) *Reflective Teaching and Learning in Further Education.* Northwich: Critical Publishing.

Barentsen, J R and Malthouse, R (2013) *Reflective Practice in Education and Training.* London: Learning Matters.

Bassot, B (2013) *The Reflective Journal.* Hampshire: Palgrave Macmillan.

Moon, J (2006) *Learning Journals: A Handbook for Reflective Practice and Professional Development.* Oxon: Routledge.

Rushton, I and Suter, M (2012) *Reflective Practice for Teaching in Lifelong Learning.* Berkshire: Open University Press.

References

Atkins, S and Murphy, K (1994) Reflective practice. *Nursing Standard.* 8 (39): 49–54.

Brookfield, S (1995) *Becoming a Critically Reflective Teacher.* San Francisco: Jossey-Bass.

Dewey, J (1933) *How We Think: A Restatement of the Relation of Reflective Thinking to the Educative Process.* Boston: D.C. Heath.

Gibbs, G (1998) *Learning by Doing: A Guide to Teaching and Learning Methods.* Oxford: Further Education Unit, Oxford Polytechnic.

Johns, C (1995) Framing Learning Through Reflection within Carper's Fundamental Ways of Knowing in Nursing. *Journal of Advanced Nursing.* 22 (2): 226–34.

Kolb, D (1984) *Experiential Learning: Experience as the Source of Learning and Development.* New Jersey: Prentice Hall.

Moon, J (2004) *A Handbook of Reflective and Experiential Learning. Theory and Practice.* London: Routledge.

Rolfe, G, Freshwater, D and Jasper, M (2001) *Critical Reflection for Nursing and the Helping Professions.* Basingstoke: Palgrave.

Schön, D (1983) *The Reflective Practitioner. How Professionals Think in Action.* New York: Basic Books.

9 Measuring impact

Chapter aims

This chapter helps you to:

- understand what is meant by 'impact' and 'measuring impact';

- identify ways in which the impact of your personal tutoring core skills and key activities can be measured at both an individual and institutional level;

- understand what is meant by quantitative and qualitative measures of impact;

- identify reasons for measuring impact;

- recognise some of the issues with measuring impact;

- consider some of the many factors that influence learner performance – performance in terms of retention, success, attendance and punctuality, value-added and internal progression – and the relative importance of your personal tutoring core skills and key activities in comparison with these factors.

Introduction

Measuring impact tends to be most commonly talked about by managers and leaders, so you may not feel much ownership of how the impact of your personal tutor role is measured. By showing you the value of measuring impact and how it can be carried out at an individual level, this chapter aims to provide you with that ownership. Firstly, however, let's turn our attention to definitions.

What do we mean by impact and measuring impact?

What do we mean by impact? 'An effect' and 'influence' are likely to be included in most answers. Markless and Streatfield (2006, p 1) use the following definition of impact: '*any effect of the service (or of an event or initiative) on an individual or group*'.

Impact is defined by the Research Excellence Framework (REF) as '*"reach" and "significance" and can encompass the "effect on, change or benefit to the economy, society, culture, public policy or services, health, the environment or quality of life"*' (Research Excellence Framework, n.d., online).

We tend to associate impact with change for the good. However, it can be positive or negative and for that matter can be intended or unintended and direct or indirect (AMOSSHE, 2011, p 9).

It's also easy to confuse with other ideas:

> *There is a tendency to confuse impact with customer/student satisfaction. Customer satisfaction focuses on measuring whether or not students **like** or are **happy** with the educational experience and services they receive. Impact, however, is aimed at measuring whether or not the educational experience/service is making any **difference** to what they do and how.*
>
> (AMOSSHE, 2011, p 9)

So, when it comes to impact there is a necessary emphasis on *change*. Therefore, measuring impact needs to be measurement of change, and a comparative element over time is needed.

How we measure is also highly important, as you will see in this chapter. It's not a simple process either, and it needs thought behind it:

> *Customer satisfaction is relatively easy to measure... Impact, however, is more difficult to measure. Impact is about change, which implies that a situation needs to be evaluated before an action to stimulate change takes place, and after to determine whether indeed change has taken place.*
>
> (AMOSSHE, 2011, p 9)

Moreover, as we will see later in the chapter, the impact of activities, strategies and processes are difficult to 'prove' given other factors that can influence change.

Self-assessment is a related and relevant term. This chapter is concerned with measuring impact on the learner and this directly informs self-assessment. For example, a departmental self-assessment report ('SAR') usually contains sections on outcomes for learners and includes analysis of any equality gaps (outcomes differentiated by learning difficulty and disability, gender, ethnicity and, sometimes, economic disadvantage). In turn, information that you get from the departmental SAR may inform your measuring of impact. For example, the SAR could identify an equality gap, leading you to measure the impact of particular support measures for the group that is underperforming.

The SAR likely contains other areas such as 'contribution' (value for money) and 'leadership and management', whereas this chapter focuses on measuring the impact of personal tutoring processes on outcomes for learners. Moreover, despite the use of the word 'self', confusingly, self-assessment usually refers to processes at departmental or institutional level. It often relates to an end-of-year process involving discussion with teachers and personal tutors but overseen by managers. Depending on the approach, this could be seen as very useful or just a form-filling exercise, and all of the degrees in between! So, further subtle distinctions come from the fact that this chapter relates to an ongoing process of measuring impact and includes how to do so at an individual level. Reflection (the subject of Chapter 8) may include aspects of measuring individual impact or may be an outcome of it.

The relationship between self-assessment and measuring impact and the subtle differences between them are shown in Figure 9.1.

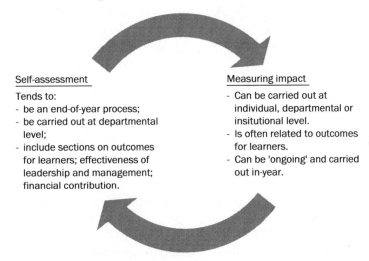

Self-assessment

Tends to:
- be an end-of-year process;
- be carried out at departmental level;
- include sections on outcomes for learners; effectiveness of leadership and management; financial contribution.

Measuring impact

- Can be carried out at individual, departmental or insitutional level.
- Is often related to outcomes for learners.
- Can be 'ongoing' and carried out in-year.

Figure 9.1 *Self-assessment and measuring impact*

What can be measured in relation to personal tutoring and how can it be done?

Here's a reminder of our definition of the personal tutor:

> *The personal tutor is one who improves the intellectual and academic ability, and nurtures the emotional well-being, of learners through individualised, holistic support.*

Critical thinking activity 1

1. List all the ways in which you think the following two parts of the definition can be measured:

   a. intellectual and academic ability;

   b. emotional well-being.

2. What do you notice about the two parts and the ways of measuring them?

Discussion

It is likely that it was easier for you to answer question 1a, about how intellectual and academic ability can be measured. Among the answers could be:

- exam results;
- success rates;
- value-added.

More difficult is deciding how to measure the second element, emotional well-being. In part, this is because you first have to decide what is meant by emotional well-being, and this tends to be subjective in nature. Aspects of emotional well-being often include the following:

- confidence;
- motivation;
- self-esteem;
- resilience;
- satisfaction.

Although this is not the appropriate place for a detailed discussion about the subtle distinctions between these aspects, think for a moment about what you feel they are. It's also worth briefly acknowledging here the complexity of the aspects themselves. Confidence, for example, according to Norman and Hyland (2003, p 6) has three elements: '*"cognitive" is a person's knowledge of their abilities; "performance" is their ability to do something; and "emotional" is feeling comfortable about the former two aspects*'.

Emotional well-being is linked to good mental health, and the measuring of this is helped by knowing more commonly accepted notions of what 'good mental health' looks like. The mental health foundation, for example, defines it as '*the ability to learn; feel, express and manage a range of positive and negative emotions; form and maintain good relationships with others; cope with and manage change and uncertainty*' (Mental Health Foundation, n.d., online).

Returning to the ways in which emotional well-being can be measured, this will need to concentrate on learners' *perceptions* of how they feel in relation to the aspects previously mentioned, which are:

- confidence;
- motivation;
- self-esteem;
- resilience;
- satisfaction.

The reason why it needs to be *perceptions* is because these are subjective topics. For example, if a learner rates themselves as nine out of ten for resilience, this does not necessarily mean they *will be* highly resilient if suddenly faced with adversity; rather, it means they *perceive* themselves as highly resilient.

Methods to measure emotional well-being could include gathering information from:

* results of questionnaires using a graphic rating scale (a system using points on a scale; a common example is zero (strongly disagree) to five (strongly agree)) on these aspects;

* the use of scaling (rating of one to ten) in one-to-one structured conversations with learners where they decide where they are on this scale related to these aspects (see Chapter 6 for further guidance);

* feedback within learner focus groups.

It's important to remember the point that measuring impact is about change, and thus comparison and timescale are needed (this is discussed in more detail later in the chapter). So, the previous examples could be carried out three times – at the beginning, middle and end of a realistic time range (for example each term or over an academic year).

Qualitative and quantitative measures

What did you notice about the different ways of measuring the parts of the definition of the personal tutor? It is noticeable that the measures of intellectual and academic ability tend to be statistical (also referred to as 'quantitative' or 'hard' measures) whereas the measures of emotional well-being tend to be non-statistical ('qualitative' or 'soft' measures). Although there can be statistics involved in the measuring of emotional well-being (for example results of questionnaires using a graphic rating scale), they are on more subjective topics, and thus the data is arguably 'softer'. Furthermore, the question of how honest learners' responses will be (sometimes referred to as 'observational bias') needs to be taken into account. This is another reason why such strategies should concentrate on learners' perception of these aspects rather than assuming any absolute 'truths'. However, this doesn't mean there is no point in measuring a factor such as emotional well-being. Often, the number given by learners when asked to scale their feelings for example, is not as important as where the learners think they are since it gives a jointly agreed point from which to work.

Moreover, the line between 'hard' and 'soft' is not necessarily as distinct as we might imagine.

> They [soft outcomes] *are used to describe gains in confidence and self-esteem, and might also include acquisition of so called soft skills, such as problem solving skills. They are usually seen as intangible and difficult to quantify and therefore different to hard outcomes which are viewed as tangible evidence of success, for instance accreditation or completion of a course of study. In practice, as Ward and Edwards [2002] contend, the distinction between hard and soft outcomes is not so clear cut, as even hard outcomes 'are often dealing with degrees of success rather than clearly defined absolutes'.*
>
> (Dutton *et al.*, 2004, p 56)

We have given intellectual and academic ability and emotional well-being equal weight in the definition of the personal tutor because, arguably, they are of equal importance to the personal tutor role or, more accurately, they are often strongly linked. In your role as a personal tutor you will be able to see how emotional well-being affects, both positively and negatively, the academic progress of your learners.

Research has shown a strong link between learning and emotional well-being as a two-way process. The report quoted above was produced after research into learners' and practitioners' views on the development of confidence – closely connected to emotional well-being as we have seen – in relation to learning. It states the following in its comprehensive review of literature on the topic: '*Confidence and self-esteem are complex concepts but seeking to understand them in relation to the learning context is important as developing them can bring about enormous benefits for learners*' (Dutton *et al.*, 2004, p 15).

Throughout this book we hope you have seen ways to have a positive effect on learners' emotional well-being which will improve their performance. As suggested by the research previously mentioned, improved learning (included within performance), in turn, improves confidence, producing a positive cycle that is beneficial to all.

> *The research findings revealed a high degree of consensus of views of the relationship between confidence and learning and the indicators and manifestations of this. … almost all the learners experienced successful learning and their confidence increased. This in turn enhanced their achievements and progression to further learning, but the combination of new skills and knowledge with enhanced confidence and self-esteem brought many broader benefits.*
>
> (Dutton *et al.*, 2004, p 31)

Due to external pressures on an institution, for example by Ofsted and league tables, the focus of the institution may be more on academic progress than the emotional well-being of its learners. However, as shown in the Introduction and Chapter 7, Ofsted has an increasing interest in the social aspects of learner progress. Moreover, the implications of the above research are that if confidence has a significant effect on both learning and learners' lives, the question of whether this should be used as an intended outcome of learning programmes needs raising (Dutton *et al.*, 2004, p 56). The reason confidence and emotional well-being are not outcomes in the way that retention and achievement are for example, is likely to be that they are seen as intangible and subjective (Dutton *et al.*, 2004, p 56). However, as such studies and this chapter show, there are ways of capturing and measuring such areas. The Dutton research proposes that developing confidence should be an integral part of initial teacher training and training for existing tutors (Dutton *et al.*, 2004, p 58).

Nevertheless, currently, if the concentration is on the academic side and success rates in your institution, it may mean it's down to you to focus on both aspects of your personal tutor role.

Why measure impact?

Think about the agreed actions resulting from your team meetings which have been carried out during the year. If the question 'what was the impact on learners?' was asked, what kind of answers do you think there would be? What do you think the effect would be if the question was asked of these actions more often or even all the time? These questions highlight to us the need to keep the learner uppermost in our minds. This can be forgotten at times, but meaningful measuring of impact, with the focus firmly on the learner, should limit this.

Sometimes the desire to measure impact is obsessional and institutions seem to measure everything that moves and breathes! Usually this situation, or perception, exists because the purpose of measuring has not been communicated clearly, or there is a lack of clarity over what particular aspect is being focused on. Many of us can think of occasions when we've been asked to provide statistics without being told how these statistics will be used. Without this clarity, it can be easy to become disillusioned with measuring impact and not feel any ownership of the process.

Moreover, it is worth remembering a maxim from William Bruce Cameron, '*Not everything that can be counted counts. Not everything that counts can be counted* [measured]' (Cameron, 1963). You need to avoid measuring for the sake of it without a specific purpose. Likewise, you need to accept that certain things are important but are difficult to measure or, indeed, don't need measuring.

Going back to why we should measure though, we have mentioned how exam results, success rates and value-added tend to be the main measures of intellectual and academic ability. The filtering of these by ethnicity, gender, learning difficulty or disability, and economic disadvantage to give us a picture of whether 'equality gaps' exist also provides measures of interest and use to the personal tutor since your work relates to these areas significantly.

Measuring the impact of the personal tutor at individual and institutional levels

Critical thinking activity 2

1. List all the ways in which you individually measure your impact.

2. State why you do this for each.

Discussion

1. It is likely you will have come up with some answers that are informal and everyday, for example:

   • checking verbally with learners how they are getting on;

   • checking verbally with learners how they are feeling;

   • observing learners' mood;

   • observing learners' engagement.

More formal and longer-term examples might include:

- carrying out 'intervention analysis': monitoring attendance and completion of work levels of particular learners who have been the subject of specific personal tutoring actions of yours; this intervention analysis can be carried out in-year (monthly) or end of year and can analyse changes over time and trends;

- comparing the number of formal disciplinaries or behavioural incidents with your cohort of learners before and after you have used a positive approach to disciplinary, for example positive learning conversations;

- analysing how many of your learners did not have positive 'destinations' the previous year and focus on reducing the number for the current academic year through targeted support on progression.

The measures will be a mixture of qualitative ('soft') and quantitative ('hard').

You may be thinking that the list of what and how you can measure is endless. If so, good, this is exactly how it should be! On the more formal side, you can measure the impact of multiple variables. In a sense, this also answers our earlier question about what is worth measuring. We can't know this until we actually measure it! We ought not to be afraid about choosing the most 'random' or seemingly small or insignificant variable. I once observed a mathematics lesson where the teacher used to play a song at the beginning of each lesson. When she didn't do this one week the learners complained saying they really wanted to know each week what the song would be. An interesting impact analysis of the use of a song at the beginning of the lesson on learner punctuality and attendance could be carried out here.

It's also important to note that you have greater freedom at the individual level. You don't need to wait to be asked to do so by your manager or the institution, you can look at the impact of variables that you yourself think may have an impact (using both quantitative and qualitative measures). Taking your methods and results to your manager might even result in them being used by others for the wider good of learners, peers and the institution.

2. There are two main reasons for measuring your individual impact:

- to check whether what you are doing helps your learners (in terms of their learning, progress, motivation and well-being);

- to ensure your personal tutoring practice is improving.

At the institutional level, the focus is on key performance indicators (KPIs) including retention, success, attendance and punctuality, value-added, internal progression and, increasingly, destinations of learners. At the individual level, the measure that the variable has an impact on, particularly the quantitative ones, will often be the same as one or more of these KPIs. In the example of the seemingly unusual variable of the use of a song at the beginning of the lesson, the KPI of attendance could be the measure of impact. The greatest impact institutionally will be seen if individual practice (shown to positively affect a KPI at an individual level) is consistently applied by the institution through awareness, training and joint practice development. Your individual measuring of impact thus has a strong link to, and influence on, the institutional measuring of impact and thus institutional performance.

How you measure impact

Personal tutor impact measures

Remind yourself of the personal tutor core skills and key activities and procedures (target setting also included). Concentrate on the following.

* one-to-one conversations with learners (including solution-focused coaching techniques);
* group tutorials;
* the tracking and monitoring of learners;
* disciplinary – a positive approach;
* target setting;
* right course review.

Critical thinking activity 3

1. What are the best ways of measuring the impact of these on learners' intellectual and academic progress and emotional well-being?
2. Who will carry out this measuring?
3. What are the success criteria for each and where will the evidence be found?

Discussion

Look at the suggested answers in Table 9.1.

Table 9.1 *Measuring the impact of the personal tutor core skills and key activities and procedures*

Personal tutor core skills/key activities and procedures	How could impact be measured? (Repeated over a particular timescale)	Who carries out the measuring?	Where will the evidence of impact be found? What are the success criteria? (Comparison within a timescale needed)
One-to-one conversations with learners (including solution-focused coaching techniques).	• Observation (both peer and formal). • Quality audit on one-to-one recording. • Learner satisfaction surveys. • Informal discussions with learners.	• Line manager. • Peers. • Personal tutor.	• Feedback from peers and manager. • Quality audit results and report on elements of effective one to ones. • Survey results and feedback. • Key performance indicators: • Retention rates. • Success rates. • Attendance and punctuality rates. • Value-added scores. • internal progression rates.

Table 9.1 *(cont.)*

Personal tutor core skills/key activities and procedures	How could impact be measured? (Repeated over a particular timescale)	Who carries out the measuring?	Where will the evidence of impact be found? What are the success criteria? (Comparison within a timescale needed)
Group tutorials.	• Observation (both peer and formal). • Learner satisfaction surveys. • Informal discussions with learners.	• Line manager. • Peers. • Learners. • Personal tutor.	• Feedback from peers and manager. • Survey results and feedback.
The tracking and monitoring of learners.	• Quality audit on tracking and monitoring recording. • At-risk meetings with manager. • Individual 'intervention analysis'.	• Line manager. • Personal tutor.	• Quality audit results and report on elements of effective tracking and monitoring. • Feedback from the manager in at-risk meetings. • Key performance indicators (listed previously) with particular attention to learners at high risk where specific support actions have taken place.
Positive learning conversations (PLCs).	• Observation (both peer and formal). • Quality audit on PLC recording.	• Line manager. • Peers.	• Feedback from peers and manager. • Quality audit results and report on elements of effective PLCs. • Key performance indicators (listed previously) of learners who have had PLCs.
Target setting.	• Quality audit of recording of processes which include target setting – one-to-ones, tracking and monitoring, PLCs.	• Line manager.	• Quality audit results and report on feedback on the extent to which targets are 'SMART' and 'stretch and challenge' learners. • Key performance indicators (listed previously) with particular attention to value-added scores.
Right course review	• Observation of right course review one-to-ones. • Quality audit of the right course review process.	• Line manager.	• Feedback from manager. • Quality audit results and report on elements of successful right course review. • Internal progression rates. • Percentage of transfers (movement of learners from one course to another). • The remaining key performance indicators (listed previously).

The list is not exhaustive and other ways of measuring could be included (see also 'informal' measures in the discussion of Critical thinking activity 2).

It's important to note that we have listed the principal person responsible for carrying out these actions in the third column, but we could easily have added the personal tutor in each case.

In the fourth column we have frequently mentioned quality audit results and reports. The *results* will inform you whether the action has taken place, for example that the minimum required number of one-to-ones per term have been completed. The *reports* on the relevant activities (for example one-to-ones) will inform you of the quality of the elements of each activity. An audit report should include reporting on the following elements:

- detail;
- knowledge of learner;
- use of solution-focused techniques, for example scaling;
- target setting and the extent to which the targets are SMART.

The importance of comparison and timescale

You will notice the mention of timescale and comparison within the titles of the second column (how could impact be measured?) and the fourth column (where will evidence be found and what are the success criteria?). These need to be taken into account in order to measure change and thus impact. Key performance indicators tend to have this built in as in-year and end-of-year measures. Longer-term trends can be important. For example, if there is a slight decrease in a KPI(s) from one year to the next but the overall trend since a particular support strategy was brought in (for example over three years) shows a significant increase, there is an indicator of positive rather than negative impact. Viewing the end-of-year figure compared to the previous year in isolation would have suggested the opposite.

When it comes to learner satisfaction surveys, the article quoted in the introduction to this chapter stated that they are not measures of impact since measuring whether learners *like* or are *happy* with their educational experience (in our case, personal tutoring) is not the same as whether it has made any *difference* (AMOSSHE, 2011). However, this can be addressed in two ways. Firstly, carrying out surveys over a timescale – ideally at the beginning, middle and end of a process – gives you comparative data to measure change. Secondly, focusing the questions of the survey on learners' perception of their progress in relation to a specific variable (examples include coaching techniques such as scaling or a behaviour management strategy) rather than what they like or dislike can give you a clearer indication of change in the areas we are interested in: learners' progress and emotional well-being, rather than 'satisfaction'.

Using the National Occupational Standards

Historically, learner support hasn't been provided with the standards against which to measure quality, and thus to measure impact. It is traditionally associated with the emotional well-being side of the learner, and so 'softer' measures have been used. However, the recently established National Occupational Standards (NOS) in Personal Tutoring can provide a starting point to consider how to measure the impact of your actions.

These give a comprehensive overview of the aspects of the personal tutoring role and are a useful set of benchmarks against which to measure the quality of your role as a personal tutor. They are not an impact measure in themselves but can be used as a way into doing so and for you individually to self-assess your skills (FETN, 2013, p 4). Broadly, if you meet all of the standards well, it's very likely a positive impact on your learners will be seen. There are 11 standards covering the following.

1. *Manage self, work relationships and work demands.*

2. *Develop own practice in personal tutoring.*

3. *Create a safe, supportive and positive learning environment.*

4. *Explore and identify learners' needs and address barriers to learning.*

5. *Enable learners to set learning targets and evaluate their progress and achievement.*

6. *Encourage the development of learner autonomy.*

7. *Enable learners to develop personal and social skills and cultural awareness.*

8. *Enable learners to enhance learning and employability skills.*

9. *Support learners' transition and progression.*

10. *Provide learner access to specialist support services.*

11. *Contribute to improving the quality and impact of personal tutoring and its reputation within own organisation.*

(UK Commission for Education and Skills, n.d., online)

Each has its own 'knowledge and understanding' and 'performance criteria' descriptors. Impact measures can be linked to specific aspects of personal tutoring performance by using the performance criteria descriptors as shown in Table 9.2.

Table 9.2 *Linking impact measures with a selection of the National Occupational Standards for Personal Tutoring*

NOS Standard	NOS performance criteria	Relevant impact measure
LSIPTO2 Develop own practice in personal tutoring.	P12 Assess the extent to which own practice is inclusive and promotes equality and diversity.	Retention filtered by gender, ethnicity, learning difficulty and disability to check for any 'equality gaps'.
LSIPTO3 Create a safe, supportive and positive learning environment.	P16 Provide tutorial support in an environment where learners feel safe, secure, confident and valued.	Learner survey results and feedback on tutorial focusing on learners' perception of their safety, security, confidence and how valued they feel as a result of tutorial.

Table 9.2 (cont.)

NOS Standard	NOS performance criteria	Relevant impact measure
LSIPT04 Explore and identify learners' needs and address barriers to learning.	P26 Communicate regularly with each learner in order to identify at-risk indicators.	Individual 'intervention analysis' of attendance and completion of work levels of particular learners who have been the subject of specific personal tutoring actions of yours; can be carried out in-year (monthly) or end of year.
LSIPT09 Support learners' transition and progression. (UKCES, n.d., online)	P63 Work with learners to identify, where appropriate, goals relating to their career development and suitable and realistic progression options. (UKCES, n.d., online)	Internal progression rates for your learner groups. Analysis of destination data for your learner groups.

Critical thinking activity 4

» Read the performance criteria from the whole set of standards and choose two criteria from each of the 11 (without repeating those chosen previously) and, as shown in the final column of Table 9.2, give a relevant measure of impact for each criterion.

Being constructively critical of measuring impact

The adage 'you can't fatten a pig by weighing it' famously came from educator Carolyn Chapman in the world of American primary education, referring to the over-testing of children at the expense of actually educating them. In other words, 'we aren't feeding kids' minds when we are assessing them' (Weuntsel, 2011, online). We can widen the idea to remind us of the dangers of over-measuring. Is too much time and effort spent on measuring, meaning that the actual job at hand suffers?

Many teachers may also feel that in recent years there has been an imposition of quality criteria (which are more often than not impact measures) on education and training institutions which were originally related to a profit-making commercial context (Gravells and Wallace, 2013). They may point, quite rightly, to the fact that quality outcomes of an educational institution are different to those of a factory for example (Gravells and Wallace, 2013). Some would also point to differences between 'learner' and 'customer', a debate for another time. Albeit talking about higher education institutions, The Association of Commonwealth Universities makes a similar point:

> *For universities it is important too, though, that their work – education and research, and what flows from it – is properly understood, so that institutions are not expected, to respond with greater yield in the same way as a production line might if given greater input. Before any measures or judgements of impact can be made, the values and goals which underpin educational investments need to be clarified and made explicit.*
>
> (The Association of Commonwealth Universities, 2012 online)

In other words, even if more 'input' (for example funding) is given, greater 'yield' (for example positive impact) should not be expected without question. Rather, values and goals need careful thought first.

How many times have you heard a sportsperson or commentator say 'the score doesn't tell the whole story'? (Weuntsel, 2011, online). When it comes to statistical or hard measures you need to remember the issues beneath this headline data and that any thorough analysis of impact acknowledges these. With attendance rates for example, several factors, alongside personal tutor actions, play a part in contributing to these, both negatively and positively.

Acknowledging other factors that influence learner performance

Critical thinking activity 5

The main key performance indicators relating to the personal tutor role are retention, success, attendance and punctuality, value-added and internal progression.

1. Choose two of these indicators. For each, with the indicator in the middle, draw a spider diagram showing what you think all of the factors are which influence (a close synonym for 'impact') learners' performance in this area.

2. Think of two of your learners. Estimate what percentage of influence your personal tutor practice has (relative to the other influences) on your chosen key performance indicators for each learner and why.

3. Has this influence changed since you first started working with each of them?

Discussion

1. As I'm sure you have found, the factors are multiple. This shouldn't be any surprise, since, like all people, learners are complex entities! Retention rates alone may be affected by a number of things, as shown by the example spider diagram in Figure 9.2.

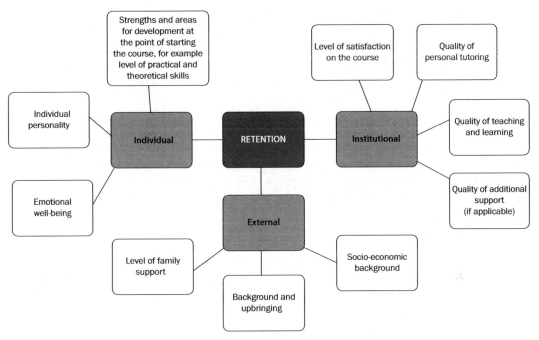

Figure 9.2 *Factors that influence retention of learners*

This list is by no means exhaustive. As you can see, our example answer has naturally fallen into three types: *institutional*, *external* and *individual* factors. You may also notice that the influencing factors are relevant to more than one performance indicator; they are relevant influences on attendance rates, for example.

2. You have no doubt found that the estimated percentage varies depending on which learner you have in mind. Even considering one learner, this is not an exact science due to the complex nature of individuals. However, it is always useful to assess the extent of our influence. If the estimated percentage was low for a particular learner, focusing on the significant influences helps you to understand what makes that learner 'tick' and you can adapt your strategies accordingly to tap into this, for example by establishing rapport through conversation and showing interest in their interest or 'passion'. This way your actions are working with, rather than against, other influences.

3. This question is always important to ask since measuring impact is about measuring change and it cannot be done without considering timescale and using comparison within this timescale. Even if your estimated percentage of influence for a learner is low, the important consideration is whether it has changed (hopefully increased!) since you first started working with them.

When it comes to retention, it is interesting to note that since funding is partially linked to it, in the eyes of the government, it is institutional factors that are most important rather than external and individual ones, a bone of contention among some teachers and personal tutors. They may argue that it is unfair to be judged on these criteria for all learners since there are certain things which are simply outside their control. However, Martinez's (2001, p 3) summary of research shows that learners who 'drop out' are not strongly differentiated from learners who complete in terms of their personal circumstances, such as personal, family or financial difficulties, their travel costs and ease of journey into college.

Correlation and causation

There is not a straight causal line between your practice and learner performance, which means that direct impact is not easy, or even possible, to 'prove'. However, this is no different from anyone else trying to measure the impact of activities, strategies or processes. Markless and Streatfield (2006) explain that the best that can be achieved with any measuring of impact is to find 'strong surrogates' for impact that provide a close approximation.

You need to remember that *correlation* is not the same as *causation*; in other words there is certainly a correlation (connection) between personal tutor practice and learner performance (as embodied in these indicators) but that the former doesn't always have a direct causal relationship with the latter. It is more important to ask to what extent your actions and support have an influence and in what ways this could be increased. By carrying out the measures outlined in this chapter we hope you see that your personal tutor practice initiates learners exhibiting improved performance and emotional well-being, 'strong surrogates' for your impact in this area.

Summary

If measuring impact is approached in the right way, is not overdone and has a clear rationale clarifying its purpose, it should be something (like observation) which you welcome rather than fear. Moreover, this should be even more the case when measuring your own impact at an individual level since you will feel ownership of the process and you are often in the best position to measure impact meaningfully.

This chapter has shown you ways in which the impact of your personal tutor core skills, key activities and procedures can be measured while at the same time recognising that the complexity of individual learners means their progress, both academically and socially/emotionally, can be affected by a number of other factors.

Learning checklist

Tick off each point when you feel confident you understand it.

☐ *I understand what is meant by impact and measuring impact.*

☐ *I can identify ways in which the two key elements of intellectual/academic progress and emotional well-being of learners can be measured.*

☐ *I understand the differences between quantitative ('hard') information/measures and qualitative ('soft') information/measures.*

☐ *I can identify ways of measuring impact at both an individual and institutional level.*

☐ *I understand the need for a clear rationale for measuring impact.*

☐ *I know how to be constructively critical of measuring impact and acknowledge and analyse factors behind statistical measures.*

☐ *I understand how the National Occupational Standards for Personal Tutoring can be linked to impact measures.*

☐ *I can see the relationship between my practice and learner performance, along with the value of assessing the extent of this, while acknowledging that other multiple factors influence learner performance.*

Critical reflections

1. To what extent do you think there is a focus on measuring the impact of personal tutor practice on learners' performance as follows?

   a. By you, individually.

   b. By your manager, at a team level, in your institution.

   c. By senior managers across your institution.

2. To what extent do you think measuring the impact of personal tutor practice on the emotional well-being of learners is carried out in the following?

   a. Across your institution.

   b. On any teacher training course you have undertaken.

   If it is not carried out or covered, how could that be changed?

3. To what extent do you learner-facing staff at your institution perceive measuring impact as having a clear rationale and as meaningful and developmental? What could be done to improve this perception?

Personal tutor self-assessment system

See following table.

PERSONAL TUTOR SELF-ASSESSMENT SYSTEM: *Chapter 9 measuring impact*

	Minimum standard 2 points	Bronze 4 points	Silver 6 points	Gold 8 points	Platinum 10 points
Individual	I am aware of the main ways my personal tutor practice can be measured: retention, success, attendance and punctuality, value-added and internal progression.	I know the end-of-year figures for the main measures of impact at group level. I consider the different influences on learner performance relating to these measures.	I review what the main influences on learner performance are at the end of the year and this informs changes in my practice the following year.	I measure my own impact on learner performance in a variety of ways in-year and at the end of the year. Quantitative and qualitative data is used to inform my future practice.	I engage in joint practice development activities related to measuring the impact of personal tutor practice.
Institutional	Staff in my institution are aware of the main ways through which the impact of personal tutor practice can be measured.	All staff have knowledge of their end-of-year key impact measures related to their personal tutor practice.	Impact measures of personal tutor practice have a clear rationale which the majority of staff support. Staff carry out individual impact measures on this practice and are supported by managers in this.	A range of meaningful individual and team-level impact measures of personal tutor practice informs wider institutional practice.	A culture of meaningful impact measuring of personal tutor practice exists which focuses specifically on learners' intellectual and academic performance and emotional well-being.

The self-assessment system is available as a free download from the publisher's website and the authors' websites (all listed at the start of the book).

Taking it further

AMOSSHE (2011) *Assessing the Value and Impact of Services that Support Students. Final Report to HEFCE LGM Funders*. London: AMOSSHE.

Department for Business Innovation and Skills (2013) Motivation and Barriers to Learning to Young People Not in Education, Employment or Training. *BIS Research Paper 87*. London: BIS.

Jameson, J and Hillier, Y (2015) Small-scale Research: Action Research and Reflective Practice in Gregson M, Nixon L, Pollard A and Hillier Y (eds) *Readings for Reflective Teaching in Further, Adult and Vocational Education*. London: Bloomsbury.

Lawrence, D (2000), *Building Self-Esteem with Adult Learners*. London: Paul Chapman.

Lindenfield, G (1995) The Power of Personal Development. *Management Development Review*. 8 (1): 28–31.

Norman, M and Hyland, T (2003) The Role of Confidence in Lifelong Learning. *Educational Studies*. 29 (2/3).

Schuller, T, Brassett-Grundy, A, Green, A, Hammond, C and Preston, J (2002) *Learning, Continuity and Change in Adult Life*. London: The Centre for Research on the Wider Benefits of Learning.

Ward, J and Edwards, J (2002) *Learning Journeys: Learners' Voices: Learners' Views on Progress and Achievement in Literacy and Numeracy: Summary*. London: LSDA.

References

AMOSSHE (2011), *Value and Impact Toolkit. Assessing the Value and Impact of Services that Support Students*. London: AMOSSHE.

Cameron, WB (1963) *Informal Sociology: A Casual Introduction to Sociological Thinking*. New York: Random House.

Chapman, C (n.d.) cited in Weuntsel P (2011) *You Can't Fatten a Pig by Weighing It: Assessment and the Future of Teacher Education*. [online] Available at: www.marquetteeducator.wordpress. com/2011/11/12/you-cant-fatten-a-pig-by-weighing-it-assessment-and-the-future-of-teacher-education/ [accessed May 2015].

Dutton Y, Eldred J, Snowdon K and Ward J (2004) *Catching Confidence*. Leicester: NIACE.

Gravells, J and Wallace, S (2013) *The A-Z Guide to Working in Further Education*. Northwich: Critical Publishing.

Markless S and Streatfield D (2006) *Evaluating the Impact of Information Literacy in Higher Education: Progress and Prospects*. London: Facet Publishing.

Martinez, P (2001) *Improving Student Retention and Achievement: What Do We Know and What Do We Need to Find Out? LSDA report*. London: Learning and Skills Development Agency.

Mental Health Foundation (n.d.) *What is Good Mental Health?* [online] Available at: www.mental-health.org.uk/help-information/an-introduction-to-mental-health/what-is-good-mental-health/ [accessed May 2015].

Norman M and Hyland T (2003) cited in Dutton Y, Eldred J, Snowdon K and Ward J (2004) *Catching Confidence*. Leicester: NIACE.

Research Excellence Framework (n.d.) cited in The Association of Commonwealth Universities (2012), *Defining, Understanding and Measuring Impact.* [online] Available at: www.acu.ac.uk/membership/acu-insights/acu-insights-2/defining-understanding-and-measuring-impact [accessed May 2015].

The Further Education Tutorial Network (FETN) (2013) *Plenary Presentation: Towards Excellence; National Occupational Standards for Personal Tutoring.* Barnsley: FETN.

UK Commission For Education and Skills (n.d.) *National Occupational Standards for Personal Tutoring.* Available online: http://nos.ukces.org.uk/Pages/index.aspx [accessed May 2015].

Ward J and Edwards J (2002) cited in Dutton Y, Eldred J, Snowdon K and Ward J (2004) *Catching Confidence.* Leicester: NIACE.

Weuntsel P (2011) *You Can't Fatten a Pig by Weighing It: Assessment and the Future of Teacher Education.* [online] Available at: www.marquetteeducator.wordpress.com/2011/11/12/you-cant-fatten-a-pig-by-weighing-it-assessment-and-the-future-of-teacher-education/ [accessed May 2015].

10 What next?

Chapter aims

This chapter helps you to:

- identify your own progress in terms of your personal tutoring professional development, as well as set and prioritise clear improvement actions;

- identify your institution's progress in terms of its approach to personal tutoring and staff development;

- see the 'bigger picture' and think broadly about how you might influence positive organisational change.

Introduction

So, now you've reached the end of this book, what next? Whatever part of the academic year it is, try to imagine what you will be doing at work in six months' time. Consider how much of this information you will remember, or more importantly how much of it you will be putting into practice, or even better you have already embedded into your daily practice.

You may have answered, quite honestly, not very much. All too often as soon as you finish a book or training course, things that you thought were really important and would work well with your learners, in your department or institution, don't get actioned due to the day-to-day pressures of the job.

In fact it has been estimated that:

- less than half the skills and information learned in training will be transferred to the job immediately after the training session unless trainers follow up on trainee performance;

- within six months, as much as three-quarters of training can be 'lost' without follow-up;

• after one year, some employees will retain as little as 10 to 15 per cent of what they learn in training unless the learning has been reinforced afterwards.

(BLR, n.d., online)

Obviously, there are other factors that impact upon how much of staff training and development turns out to be effective and is used regularly in practice, such as institutional priorities, management buy-in, and relevance to your current practice and learners. However, experience has shown that follow-ups from a trainer are important and can be effective in achieving this desirable goal. Thinking of this book like a training course or module on a teacher training or continuing professional development (CPD) course, this chapter helps to provide this follow-up for you in order to retain the learning. It will provide you with the tools to ensure that the learning from the book ends up with you and your learners and not on the shelf.

Why retain the information in this book?

All of the activities you undertake outside your day-to-day teaching of the curriculum, particularly the support you provide for your learners through personal tutoring and coaching, have a significant impact on their academic attainment, motivation, confidence and emotional well-being. This directly supports elements of their course and intended career pathway, such as engagement, enjoyment, stretch and challenge.

Displaying your core values and skills alongside your curriculum delivery will ensure that you become a highly versatile and adaptable personal tutor who provides excellent, holistic support and learning opportunities for learners in the many ways in which you work with them. This alone will help to improve your value to your learners and the institution, as well as develop your wider employability skills for your future career. But the learning gained is also key to your institution. Consider the benefits your institution might reap if it invests in developing what has been covered in the book with all of its learner-facing employees.

Critical thinking activity 1

» *If the institution you work within invested in developing outstanding personal tutoring and coaching practice with learners, what possible positive impacts on the following typical key performance indicators would there be?*

• *Retention.*

• *Success.*

• *Attendance and punctuality.*

• *Value-added.*

• *Internal progression.*

How to retain the information in this book

You are unlikely to fully commit to taking action unless you feel ownership and a strong sense of self-efficacy. Without this, all of the learning and knowledge you have developed from this book may just feel like abstract ideas which sound good in theory but feel too difficult to put into practice. The real danger is that, in time, you may forget the techniques, put your intended development actions at the bottom of your to do list (or let them fall off it altogether) or even find this book gathering dust on your shelf at the end of the academic year, unused. Professional development is your responsibility, and to feel that real sense of ownership, firstly you need to remember your previous professional accomplishments and believe in your strengths. The second stage is easier but not always simple: you need to choose your developmental priorities and commit to doing them.

Going for platinum (not gold)!

The individual self-assessment system found at the end of each chapter has been designed to provide you with a tool to help you understand where you are now and what your next developmental level is so that you are able to plan the best way to get there. The following case study provides an example of a teacher and personal tutor who works within an FE college in a large city in the Midlands. Let's call her Karen.

CASE STUDY

Karen

Karen is an art and design teacher who qualified two years ago. She really enjoys working with her learners through her teaching but also particularly through her personal tutor role, and she feels passionate about the positive impact she has on young people's lives. She has a new and supportive head of department who is open to new ideas and is keen to improve the outcomes for learners, the quality of the provision as well as the learners' experience. Karen feels valued by her head of department who recognises the hard work she puts in and the contribution she makes to the team. Not all of her team are as motivated or put in the same level of effort as Karen.

The college she works for was recently awarded a grade three (requires improvement) by Ofsted, the same grade the college received for its last inspection. There have been a number of changes in the senior leadership team and during the recent restructure a number of teaching and support staff left. The college has an overall success rate that is 5 per cent below the national average and Karen's department's courses are 3 per cent below the national average. Value-added scores and equality gaps were also highlighted as issues within her department. The college, in general, has a high proportion of learners who haven't achieved a grade C in GCSE mathematics or English and have additional support needs.

Karen has recently assessed herself using the individual self-assessment system to understand the level she is working at and to identify actions she can take to improve. The final column of Table 10.1 provides suggested examples of how she could move up the levels.

The possible actions are only suggestions and the list is not exhaustive. Every person, institution and context is unique and therefore the actions you take to improve need to be appropriate for you and your situation.

Table 10.1 Karen's individual self-assessment

Chapter	Current level (and points)	Next level to work towards (and points)	Text from the next level that Karen wants to work towards	Possible actions (this is not an exhaustive list)
2 Core values of the personal tutor	Bronze (4)	Silver (6)	I often reflect upon the impact that the core values have on the performance of my learners. The reflections inform my personal development targets.	I will: • choose a suitable reflection model or even create my own; • make reflective practice part of my weekly routine; • consider undertaking reflective practice with a trusted colleague; • keep a personal tutor reflection log (see Brookfield, Chapter 8); • speak to my learners individually or as a group to obtain feedback on what values they think I show in my work and what impact this might have; • ask a colleague to have a discussion with my learners as a group to obtain feedback on the values I project; • ask my learners to complete an anonymous online or paper-based questionnaire; • ensure that I make my personal development targets SMART.
2 Core skills of the personal tutor	Silver (6)	Gold (8)	The core skills are reflected in the feedback that I receive from observations of my lessons, group tutorials and one-to-ones.	I will: • make a conscious effort to employ the core skills within my lessons, group tutorials and one-to-ones; • include how some of the core skills help my learners through a detailed situational analysis; • ask for feedback on specific core skills from my observer; • ask the observer to have a discussion with my learners to obtain feedback on my core skills; • develop a resource for the personal tutor resource bank as a result of my observation feedback.

3 Setting boundaries	Minimum standard (2)	Bronze (4)	I revisit these boundaries in group tutorials. Through one-to-ones and other support meetings, learners have a clear idea of these key boundaries.	I will: • (where appropriate) reaffirm the boundaries I discussed at the beginning of the academic year. I feel this would be useful to build into the general discussions I have with my group about their progress and about my high expectations for the rest of the academic year; • discuss with my colleagues or manager how I feel the boundary setting that I carry out in my personal tutor role is going. For example, if I feel that there isn't an over-reliance of a learner on my support then, I take this as a possible sign that my initial boundary setting has been effective.
4 The learner experience: key activities	Silver (6)	Gold (8)	Feedback from my learners regarding the key activities is consistently very positive. Feedback from colleagues shows they regard them as having a strong impact on learner progress and outcomes.	I will: • have individual, informal discussions with my learners at set intervals over a period of time to assess whether there need to be any changes to how I employ the key activities; • undertake peer observation of my ones-to-ones and group tutorials; • ask for feedback from my manager overseeing the at-risk meetings on my preparation and actions taken; • either undertake, or ask someone (for example a trusted colleague) to undertake, an informal quality audit of specific aspects of my tracking and monitoring activities, one-to-one recording and ask for specific feedback.
5 The learner experience: key procedures	Gold (8)	Platinum (10)	I reflect and constructively question key procedures with managers and others involved to review and improve them regularly. This is a significant factor in improving some key performance indicators.	I will: • ensure that discussion around procedures with colleagues is predominantly focused on the individual needs of the learner, while also being mindful of the institution's aims; • critically analyse and evaluate on an individual basis, as well as with my department and manager, how these key procedures in the institution work to improve my learners' attendance, behaviour, completion of work and/or the department's main KPIs (such as, retention, success, attendance and punctuality, value-added and internal progression); • ensure that this information is presented constructively, with specific examples and clear suggestions for improvement, through the most appropriate communication channels.

Table 10.1 (cont.)

Chapter	Current level (and points)	Next level to work towards (and points)	Text from the next level that Karen wants to work towards	Possible actions (this is not an exhaustive list)
6 Using solution: focused coaching with learners	Minimum standard (2)	Bronze (4)	I regularly practice the use of solution talk style questions (where appropriate) to support my learners.	I will: • trial the use of solution talk questions with learners either in one-to-ones or, if appropriate, in the classroom and/or corridor situations; • experiment individually using solution talk with one group of my learners and not with others over a period of time (I may choose to use problem talk with the other group as a clear means of contrast). Through discussion with my learners at the end of the action research, I will endeavour to find out how they felt about these approaches and conversations in relation to their intellectual and academic performance and emotional well-being. Before doing this, I will consider the ethical issues of forcing solution talk on one group who may not want or need it and depriving another group of learners who may need it. I will examine some of the points and issues raised in the BERA (British Education Research Association) ethical guidelines (BERA, 2011).
7 Observation	Minimum standard (2)	Bronze (4)	I discuss the personal tutor core skills with colleagues and my line manager as a result of observation, both informally and in appraisal. I undertake peer observation.	I will: • ask my observer for feedback on my core skills following my formal observations; • consider my feedback and, with my observer, work to identify areas for improvement and any skills or knowledge gaps. We will then turn these into SMART targets; • actively engage in peer observation where possible and ask colleagues to focus on my personal tutoring core skills.

	Bronze (4)	Silver (6)	Gold (8)	Platinum (10)	
8 Reflective practice				The outcomes of my reflective practice inform joint practice development projects with colleagues.	I will: • organise joint practice development sessions with colleagues (within and across departments) to explore the benefits that reflective practice can bring to personal tutoring practice. If I am able to make these sessions a useful and regular event, I will broaden the scope to cover other areas of practice; • facilitate a training session on reflective practice on a staff training day; • enquire if any colleagues are willing to undertake reflective practice sessions together; • explain how reflective practice has helped me to improve my personal practice when discussed in team meetings.
9 Measuring impact		I review what the main influences on learner performance are at the end of the year and this informs changes in my practice the following year.			I will: • undertake a review of what I feel have been the main influences on my learners' performance while also comparing this against changes in the key performance indicators for the academic year. My judgements are likely to be drawn from areas such as my general observations and experiences, discussions with colleagues and managers on how they feel the academic year has gone and what progress learners have made, learner surveys, observations (peer and formal) and course reviews, at-risk information and Ofsted inspection; • evaluate and decide what the key changes I would like to make from the review are and ensure these are considered in my planning (for example session plans, schemes of work, new techniques and approaches) for the next academic year.

Table 10.1 (cont.)

Chapter	Current level (and points)	Next level to work towards (and points)	Text from the next level that Karen wants to work towards	Possible actions (this is not an exhaustive list)
10 What next?	Bronze (4)	Silver (6)	I use the individual self-assessment system regularly and, for all of the aspects where I am not yet platinum, I have SMART targets to guide my development.	I will: • keep a reflective personal tutor log to inform the SMART target reviews; • always set a review date (for example at the end of each term or semester) for when I will reassess myself against all of the sections of the individual self-assessment system.

Karen's cumulative score and level

46 points/Silver level

Key

Minimum standard level = 0–19 points

Bronze level = 20–39 points

Silver level = 40–59 points

Gold level = 60–79 points

Platinum level = 80–100 points

Critical thinking activity 2

1. Using Karen's context as a guide, write your own current context. You may choose to include, but not be limited to, areas such as:

    a. your strengths and areas for development;

    b. your likes and dislikes;

    c. your future career goals;

    d. key strengths or 'drivers' of positive change within your department and the institution;

    e. areas for development or aspects that might hold back positive change within the department and the institution;

    f. current Ofsted feedback;

    g. key performance indicators such as retention, success, attendance and punctuality, value-added and internal progression;

    h. learner experience feedback.

2. Undertake the individual self-assessment system at the end of each chapter to understand:

    a. what level you are currently working at for each chapter theme;

    b. what your cumulative score and overall level is.

3. For each level identified within question 2a, write down one realistic action that you can take to move up one level.

4. Using the headings below, list all of the actions you want to take to improve (from question 3) and order them with the highest priority being number one and the lowest priority being the highest number. Ensure you include a date for completion or to review each. Priority should be influenced by factors such as the impact on the learners' intellectual and academic progress or emotional well-being, targets from your mentor, appraisal, or even departmental or institutional priorities.

Number	Action	Date by when you will have achieved this or when you will review the progress.

The bigger picture

The best personal tutors (and teachers) tend to be not only excellent practitioners, both within the classroom and working with learners in a variety of settings, they are also the ones who ask the most questions and are curious about how what they do at an individual level impacts learners and learning more broadly within their institution. We are not saying that the best practitioners have to be those who are obviously keen on promotion, but that they are individuals motivated to consistently do a very good job and have a hunger for opportunities for new learning. This can be through seeking new ways to have a positive impact on learning and learners, whether that be at an individual, class, departmental or institutional level.

This section of the book provides you with an opportunity to think more broadly about your personal tutor role and even how you might influence other colleagues and effect positive organisational change. Think about the phrase 'educational institutions don't change but people do'. Educational institutions are made up of people, you can move them wherever you like and put whatever structures, job titles, responsibilities, quality checks, reporting and communication lines in place that you want to try to improve performance, but, ultimately, *people* are the most important factor in achieving success and for the institution to become regarded as outstanding.

Like a sports team, good players can still make a poor formation and tactics work. In our opinion, if you have unmotivated, unengaged people within a fantastic, well thought out structure, this is unlikely to ever achieve outstanding results consistently. A sensible structure with good systems and processes will enable strong performance to happen, but we believe it is the people within it that ultimately create high-performing, outstanding educational institutions.

Developing high-performing people and a high-performance culture in education is not an easy goal to achieve. The best explanation we've heard yet which crystallises when the culture of an educational institution is starting to move in the right direction came from a principal who said: '*I will no longer have to always be the one asking the right questions of my staff but my staff will start to ask the right questions of each other and also of me*'.

Going for platinum as an institution

Similar to the individual personal tutor self-assessment system, the institutional one has been designed to provide a forward-thinking personal tutor, existing or aspiring manager or leader with a tool to be able to understand where their institution is now and what the next level is so that they are able to plan the best way to get there. The following case study, along with Table 10.2, provides an example of a college in London.

Table 10.2 *Everyday College institutional self-assessment*

Chapter	Current level (and points)	Next level to work towards (and points)	Text from the next level that Everyday College wants to work towards	Possible actions (this is not an exhaustive list)
2 Core values of the personal tutor	Silver (6)	Gold (8)	All staff have a clear understanding of the core values and the importance of embedding them into their day-to-day work.	I will ensure that: • senior managers talk to staff informally and visit team meetings for feedback on how we are meeting the core values and where we will need to do further work; • I will explain the benefit of institutions having shared core values in order to attempt to create an institution that feels it has an identity and that staff, learners and stakeholders are happy to be a part of; • the core values form part of the content of all staff recruitment and selection processes; • we visually display the core values in appropriate places within the institution; • curriculum and non-curriculum operational planning work, such as course reviews, departmental self-assessment reports and quality improvement plans identify which core value is being displayed through actions.
2 Core skills of the personal tutor	Silver (6)	Gold (8)	The core skills are consistently and routinely improved through varied strategies. Staff are encouraged to implement new ways of assessing how effective the core skills are at improving learner outcomes.	I will ensure that: • core skills are part of the feedback asked for in learner surveys which will directly feed into the strategy for learning; • a clear and consistent skills analysis is carried out with personal tutors, which feeds into departmental and overall institutional analysis. This information will inform professional development priorities and influence budget allocation; • personal tutors are asked about which specific skills they feel they would like to develop further and support is offered where possible; • quality processes are viewed as developmental and that these recognise the effective core skills displayed as well as appropriately challenge staff to improve where required. The institution will provide support where needed;

Table 10.2 (cont.)

Chapter	Current level (and points)	Next level to work towards (and points)	Text from the next level that Everyday College wants to work towards	Possible actions (this is not an exhaustive list)
				• observations don't 'end when they end', in other words there are procedures in place to ensure that there are supportive follow-ups to enable personal tutors to 'move forwards'; • peer and/or developmental observation processes include ways in which feedback on the core skills used with learners are discussed; • sufficient resources are allocated to joint practice development and training opportunities with a focus on the value that the core skills bring to learners' intellectual and academic progress and emotional well-being.
3 Setting boundaries	Gold (8)	Platinum (10)	A range of different types of boundaries are set by departments or support functions which are informed by learners themselves. As a result of this and other factors, learners take responsibility and are independent.	I will ensure that: • information from learner surveys is shared clearly with personal tutors in order to inform boundary setting; • boundary setting and recognition for the purpose of learner independence and staff welfare form part of the content of all staff recruitment and selection processes; • boundary setting informs observation feedback, both in terms of learner independence and staff welfare; • a culture of positive boundary setting and recognition exists within the institution, not only in classroom practice but in meetings at all levels. The latter will be ensured by clear 'rules' and purposes to all meetings which all managers responsible for chairing meetings will have as an expectation.
4 The learner experience – key activities	Minimum standard (2)	Bronze (4)	The strategy for learning is effectively communicated to all new staff and updates for existing staff are frequent.	I will ensure that: • I meet all new starters within the first two weeks of them starting with the institution and one of the areas I discuss, in broad terms, is the strategy for learning. I will make sure the institution puts a strong emphasis on a positive induction experience for all new starters;

Theme			Description	I will ensure that
			One-to-ones and group tutorials are observed alongside lessons through my institution's observation scheme.	• I appreciate the value of regular, clear communication and therefore I will establish a plan for the communication of the strategy for learning through different channels; • I appreciate the value of being 'seen on the ground' and I will endeavour to discuss the strategy face to face with as many staff as possible. I will ask for feedback and actively listen to what is working and what else needs to improve, whether I agree or not; • a strong emphasis is placed on the importance of continually improving the key activities alongside curriculum delivery skills. This will be reflected in the observation policy and quality processes of the institution; • observers are fully trained in how to assess the key activities.
5 The learner experience – key procedures	Gold (8)	Platinum (10)	The key procedures are regularly reviewed by involving all relevant learner-facing staff and a selection of learners. As a result, staff feel invested in them. There is a highly consistent approach to the key procedures across my institution.	I will ensure that: • the key procedures are reviewed on a yearly basis to ensure they are fit for purpose; • staff views will be collected in a variety of ways which will influence the shaping of the key procedures; • feedback will be given directly to the staff who contributed to the consultation to thank them for their input and tell them what ideas and suggestions were adopted and how this has shaped the procedure(s); • learners are consulted for their views on the procedures and these will be taken into account when shaping the policies and procedures; • there is clear communication about the key procedures in a useable and handy format both to departmental managers and, in turn, from them to their staff.
6 Using solution-focused coaching with learners	Minimum standard (2)	Bronze (4)	Managers actively support staff to use coaching conversation techniques (where appropriate) with learners through discussion, team meetings and appraisals.	I will ensure that: • managers include coaching techniques as a regular item on their team meeting agendas; • personal tutors are encouraged to gather learner feedback on their use of coaching techniques and for this to inform appraisal; • coaching conversational techniques are used, where appropriate, in managerial meetings at all levels within the institution, so that managers embody this approach and can support staff in its use.

Table 10.2 (cont.)

Chapter	Current level (and points)	Next level to work towards (and points)	Text from the next level that Everyday College wants to work towards	Possible actions (this is not an exhaustive list)
7 Observation	Gold (8)	Platinum (10)	There is an important emphasis on personal tutor core skills in the institution's informal and formal observation schemes. These skills and inspection feedback on them are comprehensively included in outcomes which form part of a cycle of continuous quality improvement.	I will ensure that: • personal tutor core skills (for example building genuine rapport, active listening and questioning, challenging, reflecting back and summarising) are included within the institution's observation scheme criteria for one to ones; • the institution's observers are trained in the central role of these core skills in learner performance along with how to recognise and develop them in those being observed; • observation outcomes related to these skills inform departmental self-assessment and quality improvement plans.
8 Reflective practice	Minimum standard (2)	Bronze (4)	My institution displays its commitment to its personal tutors undertaking effective individual or peer reflective practice through providing adequate time, resources and support for the process. Honest and open dialogue about critical incidents or issues is embraced as positive and developmental.	I will ensure that: • time and support is provided for personal tutors to undertake reflective practice; • training, which explores reflective practice, is offered throughout the year or on staff training days; • departmental managers, where possible and appropriate, try to encourage reflective practice to take place in pairs either within the department or with other staff from other departments; • there is a person within the institution who has considerable knowledge and experience of various aspects of reflective practice and he or she is encouraged to discuss this with staff proactively or answer questions reactively, if needed; • where appropriate, departmental managers speak to the personal tutors about what progress they feel they are making as a result of their reflective practice.

	Silver (6)	Gold (8)		I will ensure that:
9 Measuring impact	Silver (6)	Gold (8)	A range of meaningful individual and team-level impact measures of personal tutor practice informs wider institutional practice.	I will ensure that: • I encourage a culture of 'experimenting' ethically and responsibly with different variables in order to positively impact learner performance; • measuring impact is regularly discussed within teams along with innovative ways of doing so; • there are small 'action research' teams where willing teachers and personal tutors work collaboratively to examine a variable(s) or technique(s) that they feel may influence learner performance; • a range of impact measures are included in departmental self-assessment reports and quality improvement plans; • senior managers collate significant departmental impact measures and use this to inform institutional practice.
10 What next?	Silver (6)	Gold (8)	My institution is making progress against the institutional self-assessment chapter themes. My institution critically analyses the institutional self-assessment system and has adapted it to make it better and, where appropriate, more applicable to its context.	I will ensure that: • the institutional self-assessment system is reviewed and adapted to meet the aims and context of our institution, taking into account the views of as many learner-facing staff as possible; • on a yearly basis we review and critically analyse all of the self-assessment tools we use within our institution to ensure that the content and process is still useful and relevant.

Everyday College's cumulative score and level

54 points/silver level

Key

Minimum standard level = 0–19 points

Bronze level = 20–39 points

Silver level = 40–59 points

Gold level = 60–79 points

Platinum level = 80–100 points

CASE STUDY

Everyday College

Everyday College has recently been through an Ofsted inspection and was graded as two (good), improving on its previous inspection, where it was judged as three (requires improvement). The overall college success rate has improved by 5 per cent over the last two years and is now 2 per cent over the national average. There have also been improvements in teaching, learning and assessment, retention and value-added scores. However, attendance, punctuality and equality gaps still need additional focus. In general, there is a strong senior and middle management team, who are participative in their approach and are open to new ideas of working. Staff morale is good. The college is located in a deprived area and the typical cohort has a considerable number of learners who haven't achieved five grade A–C GCSEs and proportionately has a lot of learners with additional support needs.

Everyday College has recently assessed itself using the institutional self-assessment system to understand the level it is working at and identify actions to improve. The final column in Table 10.2 suggests how it could move up the levels. The actions are written from the perspective of a senior manager in, or leader of, the institution.

The possible actions are only suggestions and the list is not exhaustive. Every person, institution and context is unique and therefore the actions you take to improve need to be appropriate for your institution.

Critical thinking activity 3

Depending on your current role and experience, you may need to speak to a manager or someone on the senior leadership team to be able to fully complete questions 1 and 2. This will be valuable experience, particularly to understand these aspects more fully.

1. Using Everyday College's context as a guide, describe your own current context, referring to yourself as an existing or aspiring senior manager or leader for the educational institution you work within. You may choose to include, but not be limited to, areas such as:

    a. key institutional aims;

    b. key strengths or 'drivers' of positive change within departments and the institution;

    c. areas for development or aspects that might hold back positive change within departments and the institution;

    d. the perceived culture from an institution-wide perspective;

    e. typical learner profile;

    f. current Ofsted feedback.

2. Undertake the institutional self-assessment system to understand:

   a. what level your institution is currently working at for each chapter theme;

   b. what your cumulative score and overall level is.

3. For each level identified within question 2a, write down one realistic action that can be taken to move up one level.

   It is important to bear in mind when reading this table that we have written the actions with managerial experience behind us. If you have not had this managerial experience, you may find that the actions you come up with are less comprehensive. This is not something to be concerned with at all at this stage; the important point is to start thinking more broadly about your personal tutor role and 'bigger picture' issues, and to start identifying relevant actions.

Summary

The self-assessment systems that you have used are intended as a helpful guide for how you and your institution might continually improve. Be constructively critical of them and adapt or improve them to make them even more relevant to you and your institution.

At the beginning of this book, you placed yourself on a scale of one to ten in terms of your knowledge and practice as a personal tutor. On the same scale as before, where are you now and why?

We hope you feel clear and positive about the next steps that you can take to develop outstanding practice and that this is the beginning or continuation of the increasingly positive impact you will have on your learners and the institution you work within.

Learning checklist

Tick off each point when you feel confident you understand it.

☐ *I understand that in order for the learning from this chapter and the book to not end up on the shelf, I need to take ownership and set myself small incremental actions which I will take to improve my personal tutoring practice.*

☐ *I appreciate that all learners, staff, departments and institutions are different and that any decisions made should be relevant and appropriate for each particular context.*

☐ *I recognise the value of seeing the bigger picture because this will help me to, firstly, recognise why some decisions are made and, secondly, be able to fully understand how I can influence the institution more broadly.*

☐ *I understand that critically analysing the self-assessment systems is a good thing and that adapting them to be even more relevant and useful not only shows that I think critically about my personal tutoring practice but that I am willing to take ownership of my own development and attempt to influence the development of my institution.*

Critical reflections

1.   In relation to all of the learning from the book, identify and explain which aspect you feel:

   a.   most proud of in terms of your own personal tutoring practice and why;

   b.   you would like to develop first and why;

   c.   the institution you work within should feel most proud of in terms of its own personal tutoring practice and why;

   d.   the institution you work within should consider developing first and why.

2.   In relation to 'bigger picture' decisions that affect learners, staff and the institution more broadly, explain what you feel the three key critical success factors are which will ensure that a new idea, policy or procedure has the greatest chance of being effective.

3.   A senior manager working at, statistically, one of the top three performing colleges in Britain (at the time of writing), said to us, '*without seeing it, I know that your educational institution already has everything it needs within it to become outstanding, it is all about developing the culture and people*'. To what extent do you think that, in order for an institution to become outstanding, it is '*all about developing the culture and people*'?

4.   If you skim read this book to identify the key messages from all of the chapters, what would you identify as the top five recommendations in order to make your personal tutoring practice outstanding?

Personal tutor self-assessment system

See following table.

PERSONAL TUTOR SELF-ASSESSMENT SYSTEM: *Chapter 10 What next?*

	Minimum standard 2 points	Bronze 4 points	Silver 6 points	Gold 8 points	Platinum 10 points
Individual	I feel a strong sense of ownership of my professional development and ultimately view it as my responsibility.	I reflect and think holistically about all aspects of my personal tutoring practice. My ultimate goal is to achieve platinum in all chapter themes.	I use the individual self-assessment system regularly and, for all of the aspects where I am not yet platinum, I have SMART targets to guide my development.	I am making progress against the individual self-assessment chapter themes. I critically analyse the individual self-assessment system and have adapted it to make it better and, where appropriate, more applicable to my context.	I have achieved platinum for all of the chapter themes within the individual self-assessment system. I am now investigating ways in which I can develop my personal tutoring practice, and that of my colleagues, further.
Institutional	Generally, the personal tutors in my institution feel consulted and supported with regard to their professional development. One of our aims is to help staff take ownership of their professional development.	The majority of our personal tutors are making progress against the individual self-assessment criteria. Our ultimate goal is to achieve platinum in all chapter themes.	My institution uses the institutional self-assessment system regularly, and for all of the aspects where we are not yet platinum we have SMART targets to guide our development.	My institution is making progress against the institutional self-assessment chapter themes. My institution critically analyses the institutional self-assessment system and has adapted it to make it better and, where appropriate, more applicable to its context.	My institution has achieved platinum for all of the chapter themes within the institutional self-assessment system. We are now investigating ways in which we can sustain this level, as well as continue to develop our staff, systems and processes further.

The self-assessment system is available as a free download from the publisher's website and the authors' websites (all listed at the start of the book).

Taking it further

Coffield, F (2010) *Yes, But What Has Semmelweis To Do With My Professional Development as a Tutor?* London: LSN.

Elbot, C and Fulton, D (2008) *Building an Intentional School Culture: Excellence in Academics and Character*. California: Corwin Press.

Fielding, M et al (2005) *Research Report No 615 Factors Influencing The Transfer Of Good Practice*. Nottingham: DfeS Publications.

Gregson, M, Spedding, P and Nixon, L (2015) Helping Good Ideas Become Good Practice: Enhancing your Professional Practice through Joint Practice Development (JPD) in Gregson, M, Nixon, L, Pollard, A and Hillier, Y (eds) *Readings for Reflective Teaching in Further, Adult and Vocational Education*. London: Bloomsbury.

The above title is useful in particular for ideas on initiating joint practice development projects.

James, D and Biesta, G (2007) *Improving Learning Cultures in Further Education: Understanding How Students Learn*. London: Routledge.

Sebba, J, Kent, P and Tregenza, J (2012) *Joint Practice Development (JPD) What Does The Evidence Suggest are Effective Approaches?* Nottingham: National College for School leadership.

References

BLR (n.d.) *Reinforcing Your Employee Training – Are You Sure Your Training Program is Effective?* [online] Available at: www.blr.com/trainingtips/training-program-reinforcement [accessed May 2015].

British Education Research Association (BERA) (2011) *Ethical Guidelines for Educational Research*. London: BERA.

Index